To Eileen

with

Love &

Blessings

Julia
Deland
Keene

FROM SOAP OPERA TO SYMPHONY

Julie Ireland Keene

authorHOUSE®

AuthorHouse™
1663 Liberty Drive
Bloomington, IN 47403
www.authorhouse.com
Phone: 1-800-839-8640

First published by AuthorHouse 4/14/2010

ISBN: 978-1-4520-0434-1 (e)
ISBN: 978-1-4520-0435-8 (sc)
Printed in the United States of America
Bloomington, Indiana
This book is printed on acid-free paper.
Library of Congress Control Number: 2010903926

PREFACE

"Sharing our story can open our eyes to
the ambushes we share with others and
open paths to freedom"
- Marion Woodman

A desire to tell my story has been in my mind for years. Why has it taken so long to actually do it? During my twenties and thirties, I was so immersed in day to day soap opera crisis that I didn't have the time, energy, or necessary perspective to even begin. Later, as I became more settled and established on a spiritual path, I again thought about writing my life story "someday." I put off that someday several times. The reason has been that I still had so much remaining inner work to do. I wanted to be able to tie up the story with pretty bows and nail down a "happily ever after" ending.

However, in Earth School there is no happily ever after that guarantees no additional learning or challenges. In fact it is just those experiences and circumstances that facilitate our continual learning and growth. I believe that is the true purpose of our stay here - to expand our spiritual awareness and understanding, which results in more love for ourselves and everyone in our lives.

I finally have the understanding that I'm not finished yet, and won't be, because there is always a higher level beyond where we are. I am a dynamic ever-changing process. There is no end to our growth process. Wisdom literature tells us that there are even layers and levels in Heaven. So, with the understanding that I'm not finished yet, I will share my challenges and experiences and what I have learned from them. My sincere prayer is that you, dear reader, may be inspired to "keep on keeping on" in the process of learning and growth, to heal whatever is unhealed within you so that you may live in the joy of life that is our Divine Inheritance.

CHAPTER ONE
THE SOAP OPERA BEGINS

You have to see the whole of your past as living
and that by working now you can change the whole
of the past and all that is connected with it
—Maurice Nicoll

January 1959: He lay dead drunk on our bed, and I knew from past experience that he would be passed out until morning. As I stood over him, my habitual helpless despair faded away, and the accumulated frustrations, disappointments and abuse of twenty-seven years rose up within me and shouted, "Enough!" All emotion faded as I calmly walked to the closet and removed the plastic bag from the dry cleaning. I knew that "Warning! Danger of suffocation!" was printed on the bag. The cluster of thoughts and feelings that could be identified as my personality watched from the ceiling as the woman below approached the inert form on the bed and began to place the plastic bag over his head.

January 1941: The winter sun, shining through the lace curtained window, sent sparkles of light dancing off the blue and white linoleum. Soaking up the welcome warmth, I retreated into a private world. Here, in spite of my current bleak existence, I dreamed of how fate might intervene at any moment to make things better. It was time for my favorite soap opera, OUR GAL SUNDAY. The deep and dramatic voice of the announcer asked, "Can a girl from a small mining town in the west find happiness with the wealthy and titled Englishman, Lord

Henry Brinthrop?" I admired this soap opera heroine's valiant struggle to find happiness and a better way of life in spite of overwhelming difficulties. There was always hope for a better future.

I needed hope then because my mother's new husband seemed to hate me. Too often, I felt the sting of his harsh words and punishing belt. To add to the pain, his three children, all older than I, enjoyed making me the target of their teasing and jokes. As we walked to our country school, carrying our lunches in Karo Syrup pails, their teasing became miserable and frightening. Sometimes, the edges of their lunch pails left bruises on my legs, but it was useless to complain. Mother made some effort to protect me, but her priority was the survival of her fourth marriage.

Soap operas sometimes helped both Mother and me to escape our difficult worlds. The inevitable way out of the heroine's dilemma was to find a man who would love her and rescue her. HELEN TRENT's challenge was to find love and happiness, even after thirty-five. My mother was over thirty-five and determined to make her current marriage work. She chose to put up with harsh criticism from her husband and step-children and to look the other way when I was physically and verbally abused so that she would not have to fight the world by herself again. Because she had no special skills and could only find employment as a domestic, it had been extremely difficult for her to support us on her own. We barely survived the great depression.

On that January morning as we listened to OUR GAL SUNDAY, I did not question why Mother suggested that I stay home from school. I was just enjoying the rare peace and comfort of having her all to myself. There was no warning that my life was about to be changed as suddenly and dramatically as that of any soap opera heroine. "Honey, I need to talk to you," Mother announced as she turned the radio off and sat down beside me. "I'm not really your mother," she said softly, "but

I've always loved you just as if you were my own child. Your sister Ruth is your real mother. I'm actually your grandmother. I know you're very unhappy now, so I've found a way to make things better for you. Some people who want a little girl of their own will adopt you, and I know you will have a better life."

Because my child's mind could not grasp the significance of what I was being told, I was not devastated. Besides, I had been left with many different people and had adapted to so many changes that I felt I could somehow survive this one. I trusted that my mother loved me and wanted a better life for me, a life that she could not provide. "The people are coming to pick you up today," she said. "Your clothes and belongings are in a box and ready to go." It was all happening so fast that I didn't have time to think. Yet, dramatic as this day was, it was merely a continuation of the ongoing drama and trauma to which I was so accustomed.

My personal soap opera began when "Illegitimate" was stamped on my birth certificate on June 13, 1932, when I was born to an abused mixed up girl named Ruth, just after her own fifteenth birthday. Florence, Ruth's mother, raised me as her own until that fateful day in January 1941 when she sent me away. The lives of Florence and Ruth had begun to unravel when they both were given a venereal disease by Florence's husband and Ruth's father. At the time there were three children, Ruth, the oldest, Harry, and Beulah. When Florence left the marriage, the children were all placed in foster care.

Later, Florence remarried, and the children came to live with her. Florence's second husband Bill decided to have sex with fourteen year old Ruth and raped her. To cover up what he had done, he asked one of the neighbor boys to "initiate" Ruth into sex. As a result of this abuse, Ruth became pregnant and was sent to a home for unwed mothers over 100 miles away from any of her family. Bill told the director of the home that Ruth was a "bad and wild girl," and he and Florence never visited, although Ruth was in the home for several months. This fourteen year old girl was left to cope with her pregnancy alone. After my birth, Florence and Bill took me home with them, sending Ruth to live with her father and his new wife who would give her an opportunity to attend high school.

My memories of those early years on Bill's farm just outside of Caro, Michigan are very sparse. I vaguely remember being at Bill's bedside when he was very ill and playing with his pocket watch; he died when I was very young. My impression is that he was kind to me, although that is difficult to reconcile with his cruelty toward Ruth. Furthermore, I have huge memory gaps concerning those early years before nine; I have no doubt there are deeply buried wounds that I have not been able to access. Another experience from that time period is more clearly recorded in my memory bank: I am at the end of the farm's driveway, fascinated by the play of sun and wind on the leaves of the quaking aspen that stand guard there. Hearing the roar of a road grader, I run back to the house in a panic. Sister Beulah has warned me about the bogeyman and these roaring road monsters!

After Bill's death, Florence was on her own again, needing to work and survive, needing to leave me many places, sometimes with relatives, sometimes in foster care. I believed that Florence, the only mother I knew, loved me and was trying to do the best she could. I was often lonely, scared, confused and hungry. However, the pervasive feelings were sadness and a deep sense of inferiority. I began to suspect that something was wrong with me after I started school and realized that the other kids were different, certainly more carefree than I.

Although I started kindergarten in the small town of Caro, not far from where we lived, it was a totally strange world. Ashamed of my clothes, I felt ugly. The other children took the myriad of lovely toys in the classroom for granted and felt at home playing with them, but I was overwhelmed and knew I didn't belong. The little girls wore anklets, but I was made to wear ugly long stockings that I rolled down during school and rolled up again on the way home. However, circumstances were constantly changing. As a portable child, I was never in one school for long; I moved with my mother to wherever there was work for her, or I was left with people I didn't know in a foster home, or I stayed with relatives. There was not an opportunity to put down roots, to belong.

Yet, there were some positive experiences in my wanderings. I cherish the memory of a foster home in Sandusky, Michigan where I lived for all too short a time with a tall dark haired woman named Tess, her mellow husband and their black Scotty dog. They had a fireplace; the husband smoked a good smelling pipe, and I felt nurtured, safe, and cared for. My heart began to yearn for this "happily ever after" home as a possible permanent one, but it was not to be. No one ever explained to me why I was moved so often, so I feared that I was somehow inferior, not good enough to be someone's "normal" little girl. For a short while, I was placed with some kind people on a farm. They had children who accepted me; we played in the barn and the father squirted warm milk from the cow's udder into our open mouths. We walked barefoot through fresh cow pies. We curled ourselves into balls and rolled down gentle hills. I recall awaking in a sunlit room after a nap and feeling at peace with the world, a rare and treasured brief interlude of joyous innocence.

Sometimes I was left with Grandpa Perry, Florence's father. Grandmother Perry died of tuberculosis before I was old enough to remember her, and Grandpa lived alone on a small acreage and enjoyed tending his garden. I loved his fresh vegetables and home cooking, but best of all, I loved not being hungry. Grandpa was kind and always happy to see me, and it seemed so peaceful at his house. At the time, I was too young to understand what he was doing in the night when I was only partly awake. I was aware that he was kneeling over me, breathing very heavily and rubbing between my legs. Awhile later he would stop and wipe up something wet and sticky. He didn't hurt me, and I went back to sleep. In the morning, it was like nothing had ever happened. He died when I was about five years old, and I remember feeling sad at the time. A few years elapsed before I grasped the significance of his actions and consequently felt shamed and flawed because of them.

Two brief visits to my "sister" Ruth were a treat for me. I had no clue that she was actually my mother. After finishing high school, she moved to the Detroit area, married Jack, and had two boys. I appreciated her neat and well furnished apartment and the attention I received from her. Other times I visited my "sister" Beulah, actually my aunt, and her husband Lee. Married when Beulah was only fifteen, they had few material possessions, but obviously loved each other very much and had a good marriage. I liked to help Beulah with little Wilbur Lee, their oldest son who was just a baby. Beulah knew how I hated my straight hair and made time to wave it. The touching and attention felt good. Lee's mother, who lived next door, took time to pay attention to me too and invited me to visit her often. While I combed her hair, we both had fun pretending I was her hairdresser while we talked about God and the Nazarene church. Very religious, she told me all about a loving Jesus. Around this time Florence took me to an evangelical meeting. The beautiful blond woman preacher seemed to glow with love and looked like an angel to me. "I'll be like her and do what's she's doing someday," I promised myself.

Florence's marriage to her third husband lasted for only a short time, a disappointment because the divorce would force Mother to work again, and we would be separated. This husband's tendency toward violence manifested early. He often hit us when he was in a bad mood, which was often. When he left, we went on welfare. People on welfare were not supposed to have radios, so when a caseworker came to the house,

Mother covered ours with a big red and white checkered tablecloth. The social worker didn't question what was underneath the cloth, and Mother and I were thankful. The radio, which provided some relief from our drab existence, would not be taken away.

However, all too soon, Mother informed me that she must once again go to work. On the surface, I took news of separations calmly, accepting the necessity. No one seemed to think there was anything wrong with me being left in so many places. No one seemed to notice that I was usually hungry and that when it was bedtime, I often fell asleep on the floor, ignored. I didn't consciously understand that I was being neglected, nor did I understand the anger I was accumulating. My temper, a red hot rage, seemed to come from nowhere. When the rage began to spill out, it was impossible to stuff it back in. That's when I got in trouble.

One summer afternoon, my temper surfaced when Florence and I were visiting Grandpa Perry. It had been a thrill to ride to town in his new model A Ford and to be treated to an ice cream cone, my first. On the way home, I fell asleep in the back seat. Upon awakening, I discovered that the adults had gone into the house, leaving me alone in the car. Anger boiled up in me and flowed over; my child's mind did not consciously know why I was out of control. I walked into the house, saw a vase on the table by the door, picked it up and threw it on the floor where it broke into several pieces. Spanked soundly, I cried some of my anger out, but not all of it. I asked for my usual snack - white bread and mustard with sugar sprinkled on top. Still feeling upset, I walked out the back door and fed the snack to the chickens. Grandpa saw me do this, and spanked me again. Later, I asked for more bread and mustard, which was given to me. I fed this second snack to the chickens and was spanked once more, even harder. I certainly was not being ignored; eventually, I felt better.

Because we moved so many times and I was left with so many different people, I found ways to adapt to almost any situation. However, the most difficult period of my childhood was when I felt totally alone and abandoned in a large house in the country, a house where there was almost no furniture. Florence decided to leave me home alone while she worked. I was seven years old. I had no toys, and the house felt empty and scary, except for the radio. The fear of loneliness and abandonment that was so deeply ingrained at this time continued to haunt me in my adult life. Although I now know these fears probably began in the womb, it was in that isolated house that I first became aware of my aloneness.

From time to time, Florence's brother, Uncle Conrad came by to check on me, and he began doing the same things to me that Grandpa Perry had done at night. In the daylight, he made me watch him and touch him. He didn't hurt me, but I didn't like him or what he was doing. I asked him to please stop, but he just laughed at me. This house in the country was not only isolated, it was near a state mental hospital. "If you tell anyone, I won't come and check on you. I'll just send the crazy people after you," he warned. Terrified, I didn't tell anyone. When Christmas came to this bare house in the country, we didn't have a tree, but Santa left one toy, which I was very happy to receive - a black toy telephone. In the house alone, I could pretend that I was talking to the ladies on HELEN TRENT, LIFE CAN BE BEAUTIFUL, and OUR GAL SUNDAY.

I have no memory of other Christmases recognized or celebrated except the one just after Mother remarried for the fourth time. The country school I attended with my new sister and brothers was having a Christmas program. I had a new dress for the occasion. It had a full skirt that was fun to twirl, but the best part was the print in the dress, tiny multi-colored ice cream cones printed over a pink background. It reminded me of when Grandpa Perry treated us to ice cream cones.

But, I didn't get to keep the dress for long. I made the mistake of liking it too much. One day on the way home from school, my new stepsiblings pushed me down in a snow bank, grabbed the skirt of the dress and "accidently" tore it. It felt like their mission in life was to make sure my life was truly miserable.

But a miracle was about to happen. On that fateful sunny day in January, my life's path was about to take a new turn, a turn away from the relentless atmosphere of conflict and friction. Florence had made the decision to allow me to be adopted by "nice people" who wanted a girl and who would offer me a better life. About an hour after Mother told me that she was not actually my mother, a car stopped in front of the house. The new people had come to take me away. While I waited, Florence stepped outside to talk with them. I knew my life was being radically changed, but I didn't feel excited or sad or happy. Feelings on hold, I waited to see what would happen next. I was not afraid to go off with these strangers because I trusted Florence when she said, "you'll have a better life." When she came back into the house, she had been crying. She kissed me and gave me a hug, picked up the cardboard box filled with my belongings and led me out the door. "I'll visit when I can," she promised.

The three people in the car smiled in greeting; the graying older man and younger dark eyed woman in the front introduced themselves as my new mom and dad. Their good friend Ula was with them. I rode in the back seat with her. Everyone seemed kind and reassuring as we began the 120 mile drive to my new home. While the adults talked to each other, I retreated into an emotionally numb daydream world. I was glad to be leaving my tormentors behind. I hoped that my mother would be able to cope more easily with me gone.

"Do you want to lie down and put your head on my lap?" Ula asked. I welcomed the invitation and found her soft lap comforting. The miles of electric and telephone poles and wires had a relaxing hypnotic effect as I stared up at them. I gradually fell into a peaceful sleep.

I didn't awaken until we arrived in Clare, a small town about the same size as Caro. We dropped Ula at her house, and then I saw my new home, a white two story with a big shade tree in front. Three new brothers were waiting to meet me, - identical twins, Wilbur and Willard, two years older than I, and Earl, my age. They seemed pleased to have a new sister, saying they were especially happy because now they would have someone to share the dish washing chores. I sensed this was their way of saying, "we accept you." My stomach began to relax. "Safe for now," I told myself.

The small attic room at the top of the stairs, cozy and just right for me, had slanted ceilings on two sides. The boys shared a large bedroom, but I was going to have this room to myself. It felt good to be warmly welcomed and to be treated like "somebody special." The idea that I was here to stay, not just being left for awhile, slowly began to dawn on me. Although I was almost afraid to believe that a normal life with a normal family was possible for me, I wanted it more than anything in the world. Those experiences with Tess in Sandusky and with the farm family had given me a deep desire for a loving permanent home of my own.

"School enrollment can wait until tomorrow," my new mom said the next morning. Her brown eyes expressed so much love for me from the very beginning that I had no trouble relating to her as "Mom." After breakfast the boys left for school, but Mom and I walked the two blocks downtown to shop. Walking was no hardship. We lived in the center of all important activities, - two blocks from Main Street, a block from the school, a block from the Methodist Church.

In the department store, I could barely comprehend my good fortune, which consisted of new underwear and two new dresses, one blue checked, one pink with three tiers of ruffled skirt. We stopped at the soda fountain in the drugstore for an ice cream sundae, my first. At the end of the first full day, I helped my brothers with the dishes after the evening meal and felt at home already. I felt a peace similar to the comfortable places I'd lived in the past. It was certainly a relief to be away from the violence and harsh criticism that I'd just left behind.

The next day I was enrolled in fourth grade. Although I was behind academically, the teacher was very patient and kind, and I began to make friends and adjust. However, there were still more adjustments to be made at home. My volatile temper burst forth at those times when I was incapable of resolving feelings of frustration, and during the first few months in my new home, I was easily frustrated. Perhaps I was testing the love of my new family and their commitment to keeping me. I remember throwing Mom's ironing on the floor and throwing objects at my brothers. I can't remember what provoked me to do this. Mom took the firm but loving approach, sending me to my room every time I got out of control.

Although I was making progress in school and at home, I continued to have the same nightmare I'd had for years. Snarling dogs and aggressive snakes chased me, and I woke up screaming. One night, waking up terrified, I ran into Mom and Dad's bedroom to get in bed with them for a few minutes. Usually they comforted me and assured me that the nightmare was not real, then I felt safe enough to return to my own bed and go back to sleep. However, on one evening, for the first time Mom was not there; she was out at her card club. My dad said to get in bed with him, and he comforted me about the nightmare, but he did not stop at that. He did the same things Grandpa Perry and Conrad did with me. I was still frightened about my dream and surprised he was doing these things, knowing that it was not right. This kind of molestation did not happen again, but it was not the end of the sexual touching.

Mornings, Mom liked to sleep in a little later than Dad, who was an early riser. He usually got up early and went downstairs to listen to the radio. I often needed to go downstairs to the bathroom before Mom was up, and Dad began to call me over to him for a good morning hug. The problem was that he kept one arm around me and fondled me. After a few mornings of this, the message came through to me, just as if someone were shouting in my ear: "This is wrong! Don't let him do this!" From that day on, whenever I came downstairs early to the bathroom, I hurried past the living room where Dad was sitting and pretended I didn't hear him when he called to me. Whenever I had a nightmare after that, I made myself stay in my own bed.

I didn't ever tell my mom about all this because I didn't want her to be upset. She and Dad seemed to be very much in love. His job was such that he often came home for lunch. With the school only a block away, my brothers and I were home at noon too. We often observed Mom and Dad sitting on the sofa after lunch holding hands and kissing. There was definitely something special between them, and I could not spoil this for my mother by telling her about something I had already handled by myself. At the time I had no means to analyze the situation, nor did I have conscious fears about being sent away if my father's sexual touching became known. I just wanted to protect my sweet mother who was being so kind and loving to me. Once Dad understood that I did not want him to touch me in a sexual way, he left me alone. Only much later did I come to appreciate how fortunate I was that this molestation did not continue.

A short while after the incidents stopped, the memory of the molestations and the ones before that with Grandpa Perry and Conrad faded. They were not completely obliterated, but they were buried in such a deep place in my mind that I didn't dig them up to examine them until years later. Yet, a feeling of shame remained with me. I continued to have a fear that I was defective and not quite "normal."

However, life went on in an outwardly normal manner. Positive events unfolded around me, and I began to heal and feel less alien. On my birthday, one by one my friends began to drop by until I caught on that they were coming because Mom had invited them to a surprise party for me. I couldn't believe it! I couldn't believe she had gone to so much trouble to plan a party and keep it a secret! I loved the surprise. The present from the family was a small overstuffed chair covered in flowered pink chintz. Sitting in this, I felt very special indeed and spent hours in my cozy little attic room making scrapbooks of movie stars. My brothers and I received a quarter allowance each week. Extremely star struck, I spent mine on movies, movie magazines, and paper dolls for which I designed glamorous clothing.

Many long summer days were spent with two special friends, the neighbor girls, Bev and Gerry Brown, one a year older than me, the other a year younger. We spent hours playing with our paper dolls, creating clothes and inventing adventures for them. Other times we climbed the cherry tree in their back yard and sat on the branches eating the juicy cherries and spitting the pits on the ground below. In the hottest weather we took the school bus out to the mill pond swimming area where I taught myself to swim.

About a year into this carefree new life, Florence arrived for a visit. She wanted to make sure things were working out for me. "I won't be able to visit you again because Mary and Wilbur think it's best for you if I don't," she explained. "I want you to know I'll always love you." She was crying, and I hugged her. "I'll always love you, too," I answered. I meant this, but I was feeling so good where I was that I couldn't wish to go back into my old life. I understood that we could love each other from a distance.

The true nature of the relationship between me and my new family had gradually become apparent to me. It was Florence's first husband Wilbur, my grandfather, and his wife Mary who adopted me. Although they already had three boys, they grieved over a girl who died at birth. Mary was unable to have more children and hoped I would be the daughter she always wanted. Years later, after I had grown up and wanted more details of my adoption, Mom revealed to me that Florence intended to send me to an orphanage if she and Dad hadn't adopted me. By the time I was psychologically strong enough and ready to deal with these issues, Florence had died, so I never obtained her side of the story. However, I had to wonder why she sent Ruth to live with Wilbur after he had earlier molested her, and why she sent me into the same household knowing such a thing could happen to me.

Now, many years after my experiences of sexual molestation, society has finally begun to try to come to grips with this issue, and I have come to resolution about Florence's decisions. As women's stories began to unfold, it was obvious that many, if not most mothers in these cases found a way to not recognize what was happening. I believe that many of those mothers who did know had likely been molested themselves and believed these experiences were an inevitable part of being a woman. Ruth later shared with me that Grandpa Perry molested her, and it is highly probable that he molested Florence as well. Perhaps Florence didn't know a way to make sure I would not be molested. When she sent both Ruth and me to live with Wilbur and Mary, he seemed to be happily remarried. Perhaps she felt he would not be inclined to molest - and he did not touch Ruth when she came to live with them after I was born.

In recent years, after hearing so many stories of vicious and repeated molesting, I realize that what happened to me certainly did psychological damage and has affected my life adversely, but it could have been much worse. Once I was able to make it clear to my dad that I didn't want him to touch me, he stopped. Unfortunately, most victims of this kind of abuse cannot claim such an outcome.

Thus, in spite of everything, I've given myself permission to love Florence. The child in me needs to believe that she loved me and wanted the best for me, that she was doing the best she knew how at the time. Now, my adult self recognizes that because of her own problems, she was not able to make sure I received adequate care. I can see that I should have been put up for adoption as an infant, which would have given me a chance for a better life. Eventually, I came to look at the situation from a cosmic perspective, but that would be many years and many heartbreaks into the future. After I was a grown woman, but before I had honestly looked at my childhood, I saw Florence twice, both times very briefly. I didn't ask her any pertinent questions; I just felt the need to say that I'd always continued to feel love for her, and she assured me that this was true for her as well. I didn't establish an ongoing relationship because I knew it would hurt my mother Mary.

After the short visit with Florence that day in Clare when we said our goodbyes, my child's life went on as usual. Gradually, I felt more secure with my new family. I caught up to grade level in school and made good friends. My temper was gradually fading away. My brothers and I continued to develop our brothers and sister relationship, and they delighted in teasing me, especially about a pudgy boy in my class named Glen Hardy. "Julie May loves Glen Hardy!" they would chant. I got very upset at this because Glen Hardy was the last boy I wanted to ever have anything to do with.

Another of their favorite teasing games came at mealtime. When we had spaghetti, the boys liked to talk about how spaghetti crawled around in our stomachs like worms. I couldn't eat after they said this, so Mom always made them stop. One day I asked her if they really liked me, if they really wanted me as their sister. "They really like you and want you for a sister," she assured me. "That's why they tease you. If they didn't care about you, they would just ignore you." After that, I believed they truly did like me, so the teasing bothered me less. It even started to be a fun game for me, and I began to tease them back.

During Dad's vacation time, the family spent a week in a rented cottage at a nearby lake. The boys and I loved the water and went swimming in the lake for hours at a time. We were allowed to row to the small store on the opposite shore of the lake to buy treats. At the lake and back at home, there was always something to do. When we were inside, we spent hours playing Monopoly, Checkers, and other board games. We had a croquet set for the yard, and we played wild Cowboy and Indian games with the neighborhood kids. Many winter evenings were spent at the supervised ice rink just down the block from us.

Soap operas continued to interest me in the summers or when I was kept home from school with one of my frequent sore throats. My radio horizons expanded to include The Lone Ranger, Jack Benny, The Little Theater Off Times Square, and the Hit Parade. The boys and I listened together to The Shadow and Inner Sanctum, seeing how scared we could make ourselves and each other. I was experiencing what might be called a normal happy childhood.

All this in spite of the fact that the United States was at war. Dad was over fifty years old, too old to go, but he had served in World War I and belonged to the American Legion. Food, shoes, gas and tires were rationed. Our shoes were half-soled twice before we could have new ones. We saved papers, cans, cooking oil. The newspapers and the newsreels told us about the terrible things the Germans and the Japanese were doing. We had alerts and civil defense drills, even though no one expected our small town to be a target. Yet, everyone felt they needed to be vigilant, just in case. Mom volunteered as an airplane spotter; she worked from a small room on the roof of the six-story Doherty Hotel, the tallest building in town. Twice a week for two hours, she logged in any air traffic over the area. She often allowed me to go with her, so I felt that I, too, was helping to keep us safe.

In co-operation with several other neighborhood families, we planted a victory garden which supplied an abundance of fresh vegetables and the fun of community picnics. Mom and Dad had many friends, so our house was usually lively with people playing cards, laughing and having a good time. In spite of the wartime hardships, these years were good years for me and for our family.

The local library, like most everything else in town, was within easy walking distance, and my library card opened up a larger world to me. Although I began reading fairy tales and books for younger children, which I loved, within two years I was reading many adult books, including those on etiquette and psychology. I also enjoyed the Nancy Drew series and even the adventures of the Hardy Boys. I didn't confine myself to any one subject section or age category of the library, and no one monitored the four books that I checked out nearly every week. Reading pushed the boundaries of my small home town aside and gave me access to an infinite variety of information and experiences which I found incredibly fascinating.

With so much reading and the experience of a relatively stable life, my grades at school improved dramatically, and I came to truly enjoy learning. It was satisfying to be accepted and treated like the other students, to feel that I belonged to a family and had a normal place in the larger community. "It's going to be alright after all," I told myself. Those years between nine and twelve, between fourth and seventh grades, were catching up, golden healing years. Although this relatively normal existence was about to be disrupted by new challenges, the time out from trauma was a grace period. A small but crucial corner of stability was firmly established in my psyche that would nourish me in the difficult times ahead.

Summary of Relationships:

Wilbur & Florence: children - Ruth, Harry, Beulah

Wilbur & Mary: children - twins Wilbur & Willard, Earl, (Julie adopted at age 9)

Ruth gave birth to me at age 15. I lived with Florence & with other relatives and foster care until I was adopted by Wilbur and Mary when I was nine.

Ruth married Jack: children-Jack and Ron

Ruth divorced Jack & married Ben - one son –Ben

CHAPTER TWO
LESSONS BEGIN ANEW

Life - don't analyze it.
Just get on the beast and ride.
—Marilyn Robinson

Although Dad liked his beer and whiskey, he always seemed to keep his drinking under control. By the time I was in seventh grade, he had lost control. Mom often cried by herself in the bedroom, although she never seemed angry at Dad, just hurt by his drinking. I didn't understand this. I was becoming increasingly angry that he was hurting her and hurting the family. I began to wonder how she stood him. He was twenty years older than her, and to me, a disgusting old man when he was drunk. I was unable to connect my feelings of repulsion to his earlier sexual contact with me. I thought my negative emotions were simply the result of his drinking too much. I was not outwardly hostile; I kept my true feelings to myself, and so did everyone else in the family. We were all busy trying to cope with Dad's drinking and Mom's distress over it. We didn't know how to honestly deal with our emotions, so we pretended that everything was just fine.

Then, when Earl and I were in junior high and the twins were in tenth grade, the family was thrown into a more severe crisis. After many unheeded warnings about his drinking, Dad, at sixty years of age, was fired from his job as a lineman with the power company. Even after being employed by them for many years, he would receive no pension or severance benefits of any kind. Everyone in the family needed to contribute to the family's support. I had already been baby- sitting and helping people with house cleaning on Saturdays, so I kept doing this until I was fourteen and could obtain a work permit. Then I worked in restaurants after school and weekends all through high school. Will, Wilbur and Earl each had paper routes and part time jobs in grocery stores. Mom worked as a waitress and cleaned people's houses as well. Dad managed to find work in a gas station during the times he was dried out and attending AA meetings. The family automobile had to be sold. The house was partitioned off in order to create a small apartment, which we rented out. Somehow we survived, and the twins and I managed to graduate from high school. Earl dropped out in eleventh grade, joined the army and served in the Korean War. Fortunately, he survived heavy combat duty.

These were years of extreme emotion for me. I resisted giving up the previous years' relatively normal existence. At thirteen and fourteen I wanted to fit in and be popular. I was thankful I had good friends, was pretty enough, and had a nice figure, but it was still not easy to feel okay about myself. I was self-conscious about my skimpy wardrobe. Because of our dire circumstances, I was responsible for buying all my own clothes and couldn't buy the expensive things some of the other girls had. One of my mother's friends had an older daughter who passed her discarded sweaters on to me. I was thankful for them even when they needed repair or perspiration had damaged the underarms. I envied the girls who were part of the "in group" whose parents were the town's solid citizens. During this time I made a powerful resolution: " I will make something of myself! I will be a success! I will prove to the world that I am worthy!" I felt like Scarlett O'Hara when she raised her fist in the air and swore, "I'll never go hungry again!"

I began the unrelenting effort to prove my worthiness by trying out for cheerleading. I was thrilled to be chosen as a junior high cheerleader and then re-elected by my fellow students each year clear through high school. I appreciated this confirmation that I was popular, but of course, I could never completely relax because I was afraid that it was only temporary.

Freshman year, I fell in love for the first time. He had blond curly hair, blue eyes, and a beautiful complexion; he was a happy sweet boy. His parents were very affluent, by my standards anyway. They owned a large cattle ranch a few miles from town as well as a large winter home. He had a sister who was perfectly built, blond and beautiful, and always smartly dressed. One winter evening, he invited me to his sister's home for her birthday party. Although I was full of the wonder of first love, I could not relax and enjoy the evening because I was ashamed of my threadbare coat and plain clothes. If anyone else noticed my shabby clothes, however, they didn't show it. I was excited to be invited to spend a Sunday afternoon at the ranch. During the visit, I felt like the heroine in one of the Saturday Gene Autry movies I used to love. My horse ran away, but my Hero rode after me, grabbed the runaway horse's reins and saved the day.

In December, I wore Mom's best dusty pink dress to my first high school dance, grateful for the miracle that it looked quite nice on me. I was with HIM and felt like Cinderella with her Prince Charming. It was a thrill to just hold hands. The song "Winter Wonderland" was popular, and it seemed magical to me that it indeed looked like a winter wonderland outside; my heart was full of wonder and happiness. But then it was over. I could not understand why. Rejected, I hurt terribly. He avoided me and began to date another girl. The next year he transferred to a different school. I was left with a "sorry, but you're not good enough for me" message. It was very painful, but somehow not surprising.

This "not good enough" message was further reinforced by my dad's public drunken presence. Clare was a very small town with a three block main street. Everyone met or saw everyone else there sooner or later. Of course the bars were there too, and Dad sometimes staggered home from them about the time I happened to be walking down the street with my friends. Very ashamed of him and ashamed that I was his daughter, I tried to find a way to maneuver myself and my friends into a store or across the street so I could pretend I didn't see him. I believed his behavior reflected upon me, making it impossible for me to be a "normal" teenager who fit in with my friends.

With every embarrassment, I become more determined to somehow prove my worth. Becoming involved in speech activities, I managed to perform well in spite of being nervous. I had the opportunity to travel around the state with the debate team and was a finalist in orations. Every waking moment was filled with activity directed toward my need to accomplish: major roles in the junior and senior plays, toastmistress at our Junior-Senior prom, vice-president of the senior class, and editor-in-chief of the school newspaper. All this activity was in addition to cheerleading and working and dating.

Although definitely attracted to boys, I was determined I would never get "in trouble" like Ruth did. Being "in trouble" was the euphemistic term for being pregnant. Nice girls, in these days before birth control pills, didn't have sex before marriage. I dated and "necked", which is what we called hugging and kissing, but nothing more daring than that. I had a rule and stuck by it: no touching my breasts and no hands allowed under my skirt! In spite of these restrictions, I attracted enough boyfriends that I felt satisfied with my ability to do so. I was determined to fit in with my group of peers, addicted to the idea of somehow commanding respect in spite of my dad's drunkenness. I chased away self-doubts and feelings of inferiority with a desperate effort to achieve, please, and be popular.

The high school teachers seemed to value me for myself without judging what was going on in my family. Wilbur and Will were also very good in school, popular achievers and football stars in spite of their short stature. Being the Ireland twins' sister was an asset I appreciated. The teacher who influenced me most, even though he was in the Clare system only through my sophomore year, was Richard Blanchard, the speech teacher and drama coach. He and his wife had a small baby. I felt fortunate to be asked to baby sit for them. They seemed like exotic foreigners with their New England accents, and I appreciated the books and the art objects in their home. They represented a higher level of life, and I felt privileged to be allowed in their space.

Writing speeches, reading poetry, and being in the plays were my attempts to reach for a more expanded life. I read Keat's poem "Ode on a Grecian Urn" in a classroom speech contest and won. Mr. Blanchard thought my reading was so good, he recorded it. To have a teacher I admired think my reading that special made a lasting impression on me. The prize for winning was a beautifully boxed, colorfully illustrated edition of "The Rubiyat of Omar Khayyam." I read those lines of oriental mystical poetry many times, fascinated by my first cosmic view of the world.

I wanted to place high enough in our local high school dramatic reading competition to be eligible for district competition. Very star struck, I had sent away for the catalog of the American Academy of Dramatic Arts in New York City and dreamed of going there someday. I believed that being a talented and famous movie star would be great fun; besides it would definitely prove to me and to the world that I was truly worthy. Gearing up for what I hoped would be a future dramatic career, I chose a very intense and high powered reading where Queen Elizabeth I and Mary Queen of Scots confront each other before Mary is executed at Elizabeth's command. Mr. Blanchard helped the contestants choose readings and worked with us getting them ready. My heart was set on placing well. The judges were from the town - a prominent law-yer's wife who was also a teacher, and other influential good citizens. I knew I had performed very well, but I didn't place high enough to be eligible for the district contest. Mr. Blanchard was upset. I didn't make the connection until years later that the winners just happened to be relatives of those influential good citizens. Any possibility of unfair-ness in the judging never occurred to me. I cried alone in my room for hours, but I didn't question the judges' decision. It was rumored that Mr. Blanchard talked to the school superintendent about the contest, but if that was true, I never discovered what was discussed. I was sorry when Mr. Blanchard decided to return to New England to teach the next year. My appreciation for him was great, but I would not realize the full influence he had on my life until much later.

Mixed in with all the activity, intensity and deep emotion of highschool, were also relaxing and fun times. I had close girl friends to share con-fidences; I had dates for movies and dances and times of laughter and humor. I loved to laugh and be silly with my friends, but as a result of one of those episodes of silliness, I blew a chance at a choice job. I had an interview set up with Mr. Houghton, owner of the drug store where all the kids hung out after school and where the most popular girls at school worked. Two evenings before my interview, I was clowning around with two friends, and we become more and more slap happy as the evening progressed. We began to think of all the funny things we could say to people on the phone. We tried a few numbers and asked, "Do you live on U.S. 27 ?" (the main highway through town). If the person said yes, we shouted, "Move quickly, cars are coming!" If they said no, we said, "Thank God, you won't get run over." Then we got the bright idea of calling the drugstores in town to ask if they had Prince Albert (tobacco) in the can. If they said they did, we answered, "well, you'd better let him out, he's suffocating!" I didn't think about Mr. Houghton answering the phone or recognizing my voice when I phoned his drug store and asked the Prince Albert question. However,

Mr. Houghton did answer, and he recognized my voice and informed me that the job was no longer open and why. No sense of humor! I certainly was not happy about this development, but it did not devastate me. I still had my restaurant job. I saved face by deciding that I didn't want to work for such an old "stick-in-the mud" anyway! In spite of many serious challenges during those high school years, part of me was definitely a fun loving teenager.

Mom and my brothers were loving anchors through this whole stressful time. They went about their life's business doing what they needed to do with few complaints, finding pleasure with friends and available activities. Their example inspired me to try to do the same thing. The twins finished school two years ahead of me and married their high school sweethearts soon afterwards.

The boys were all out on their own when Dad developed stomach cancer and had three quarters of his stomach removed. As a result, his insurance was canceled. In the two years before he died, and for some time after that, Mom worked extra jobs cleaning houses, trying to pay his bills and trying to survive the best she could. I attempted to feel grief at my father's funeral, but I could find no genuine tears. I couldn't forgive him for the pain he had brought the family because of his drinking. However, I did not share these feelings with anyone. I knew that I "should" grieve no matter what he had done. I also knew it would hurt Mom and my brothers if they discovered my true feelings; I did not want to hurt them, so I appeared to be a grieving daughter. Years later, I came to terms with my dad/grandfather and his actions after I discovered the healing power of forgiveness, understanding, and compassion. However, at that time, I just added my hostile unresolved emotions to the already full storage chest of guilt and shame and shoved it back into a secluded corner of my psyche.

Out of the forty graduates in my class, I placed tenth, a respectable showing considering I never took time to study outside school hours except for speech and drama projects. I graduated early in June, just before my seventeenth birthday. A limited speech scholarship was offered to me by Alma College, a private and Presbyterian school with relatively high tuition. After working and saving as much as possible in the summer, I saw that I wouldn't be able to accumulate enough to pay tuition fall term. Because there was absolutely no money from home to help me, no loans or other aid offered, I gave up the idea of attending college. In those years, at least in our small school, information was not readily available about loans or scholarships; teachers doubled as counselors, and there was not the push to get students into college that came in later years. I didn't realize that one of the state colleges, such as the one in Mt. Pleasant, only fifteen miles from Clare, would be so much more affordable than a private school. Accordingly, I looked for another path to fulfillment.

As an adventure, an attempt to push out the boundaries of my existence, I moved to Grand Rapids with a girlfriend who had graduated with me and who was at loose ends as well. We rented rooms and looked for jobs. With only a high school education, the job market was limited for us. I looked up Ruth's brother, my Uncle Harry, who lived in Grand Rapids. He and his wife worked in a furniture factory. I know they believed they were doing me a favor when they helped me obtain a job in that factory. However, the work was dirty, physically exhausting, and incredibly monotonous. Fumes from the furniture finishing were overwhelming. My job was to move unfinished tables to the sprayer and then take them away after that operation was finished. Desperate to get out of this misery, I rode the bus downtown in the evening to take some business courses at Davenport Institute. Walking the four blocks from the bus stop to the rooming house late at night was scary, but I did it anyway, determined to somehow find different employment. Although I had done well in business classes in high school, I couldn't seem to muster the necessary confidence to land an office job in the city. After two months, I settled for a job waiting on customers in a bakery. This environment was better than that of the factory, but the job began at 6:00 a.m. and required hours of standing. Although I aspired to something more challenging and gratifying than this, I wasn't quite sure how to make it happen.

Barbara, who also graduated in my high school class, was living with her Mom and working in Grand Rapids. She had a fiancee in Clare and often spent weekends there. On a spring weekend, Barbara invited me to ride back to Clare with her and her mother. We planned to take in the senior play at the high school. On that Friday evening we realized that we would need to make good driving time if we wanted to make the 8:00 pm curtain. Barbara drove her Mother's car, and we all rode in the front seat, with me in the middle. A light rain began to fall just at dusk. Running a little behind schedule because of so much weekend traffic heading north, we became a little concerned about being late for the play. We followed a slow moving vehicle for what seemed a very long time, and finally Barbara decided to pass. We were out and going around the car when it became apparent that we were not going to complete the pass in time to miss the oncoming traffic. Barbara slammed on the brakes and moved to the left shoulder of the road. The driver of the oncoming car, in an attempt to avoid a collision, also moved to the shoulder of the road, and the cars crashed head on.

I realized the cars were going to smash into each other a second before it actually happened. From a calm and quiet place within myself, a voice reassured me: "You will survive; you're going to be hurt, but you are not going to die." Then came the crunching impact, the shattering of glass, the tearing of metal. Barbara's Mom hit the windshield, cutting her face and breaking both wrists. The metal frame of the purse on my lap jabbed into my stomach and chest, knocking the breath from me.

Barbara jumped out of the car, but her legs were broken and her knees seriously injured; she fell to the ground with an agonized scream.

The screaming sirens sounded strangely comforting to me as we were rushed back to a Grand Rapids hospital. The noise reminded me that our pain and fear was being taken seriously, that help was near. After x-rays and emergency surgeries, we found ourselves sharing a room and trying to come to terms with what happened. Barbara's jaw was broken and wired shut, her legs broken and her knees seriously injured. Her Mom had 150 stitches in her face, as well as the two broken wrists. I had five broken bones in my foot and many bruises. I was the lucky one. There were two people, a man and wife, in the other car, and the wife was killed instantly. Barbara was devastated about this. We were grateful that the husband was not seriously injured. When he came to our room to see how we were doing, Barbara was so depressed about the accident and the death of the man's wife that he tried to console her. This kind man seemed to understand that he could not bring back his wife by attacking Barbara.

However, the prosecutor in the county decided to try my friend for involuntary manslaughter. I knew in my own mind that it was an accident and that Barbara did not deserve to be punished further. I felt very protective of her, one of the kindest sweetest people I knew. She was not drinking or being reckless when the accident happened. Her Mom and Dad had been divorced only about a year, and I had sympathy for Barbara's grief about that. When her Mom developed a brain tumor, Barbara put off marrying her high school sweetheart so she could help her mother through surgery and recovery. I felt very strongly that she did not deserve to be prosecuted, and I determined to do whatever was necessary to help her through this difficult time.

On the witness stand, I stated very clearly that I saw no mistake on Barbara's part and testified that the car we were attempting to pass made no effort to slow down or to prevent the accident; it may have even speeded up. Everyone who knew and loved Barbara was relieved when she was exonerated. Two years later, after the birth of her first child, she developed toxemia and did not recover. When I visited her in the hospital, although I knew that she was dying, I brought her a ceramic planter "so you'll have something to enjoy at home," I said too cheerfully. I couldn't talk to her about dying. I had to believe that she would recover. But she did not. After that, I began to think seriously about death and to realize that we can never know when it will come to us and that young people are not exempt.

After we were released from the hospital, I had no choice but to return to Clare and live with my Mom. In a wheelchair and then on crutches until the bones in my foot healed, I knew it would be months before I could do any physically demanding work. The supervisor at the Bell Telephone office heard about my plight and invited me to take the test for operator. If I passed, there would be a position for me. The telephone office was just down the street from the restaurant where I had served the operators many meals and coffee. I was touched that this woman so kindly reached out to help me. As soon as I could limp around, I took the test, passed it and was hired.

As part of the application process, I needed to present my birth certificate. Mom had my adoption papers, but not a birth certificate, so we sent to the state capitol to obtain one. I received an emotional kick in the stomach when I saw what was written on it. There was a yes or no box to check after the word, "legitimate," and the check mark was in the NO space. Of course, I knew Ruth had given birth to me when she was very young and unmarried, so I knew this information was accurate. I knew I was illegitimate and a bastard or whatever names people have called children born out of wedlock over the centuries. However, seeing it written on an official document was a further blow to my already shaky self-esteem. But I handled this disturbing incident in my usual way. I didn't talk about it with anyone and buried it in the depths of my psyche beside all the other unresolved pain.

Pushing aside this reminder of my painful past was no problem because the new job was interesting and challenging and required my full attention. I soon happily discovered that working as a telephone operator was heaven compared to back breaking labor in restaurants, a bakery, and a furniture factory. My brains were mighty grateful for this opportunity to be more fully utilized, and my body was even more grateful for an opportunity to be treated gently for a change.

CHAPTER THREE
THE PRINCE IS NOT CHARMING

Defeat may serve as well as victory
to shake the soul and let the glory out.
-Edwin Markham

From the very first moment that I laid eyes on Duane, I knew that he was The One, the epitome of my soap opera fantasies, my Prince Charming. I was with a group of friends in a restaurant one Friday night after a basketball game when three young men in uniform walked in and caught everyone's attention. "I know those guys!," one of my girlfriends declared. She excused herself, walked over to talk with them, and in a few minutes came back to our table with them in tow. I was introduced to a tall, dark, and very handsome soldier who was just returning home after two years in the army. I knew immediately that I wanted to get to know him much better.

Determined that this Robert Mitchum look alike would ask me out, I pursued him with the same energy and determination that I exercised chalking up high school accomplishments, managing to show up at the same dances or anywhere else I thought he might be. Delighted when he finally asked me for a real date and delighted when we began to go out regularly, I was not delighted that he stood me up occasionally. He would explain to me that "something came up" or admit that he "forgot," or he didn't come up with any excuse at all.

Each time I grieved and cried, but was not deterred from wanting to be with him. I had no understanding of the dynamics of this. I can now readily see how foolish it was for me to pursue such a relationship; I was asking to be neglected and abused all over again. Psychologists know that women often try to mend a painful past by attempting to change the destructive behavior of their current partner. At that time I was not in touch with my true motivation: " If I can get Duane to change and to love me and treat me well, that will make up for everything in the past." I wanted him to be the Prince Charming that would change everything, so of course, I set myself up for much heartbreak. By senior year in high school, I drank beer at dances and parties and continued to do this at times. That Duane and his buddies drank much and often didn't bother me because I believed that he was only sowing a few wild oats, having a good time, indulging in a temporary youthful fling, that he would settle down.

I met his parents, Roy and Ollie, as well as the grandparents who were very successful retired farmers and investors. His father worked in the oil industry and farmed part time; his mom had always happily stayed at home. The family was solid and respectable. I was sure that Duane, coming from this kind of environment, would turn out just fine. Roy and Ollie spent much time together and were obviously devoted to each other. This was my vision of the future for Duane and me. I truly believed that once married and once showered with all the love and wifely attentions I intended to give him, he would surely make a good husband. I observed that many other young guys settled down after marriage, and I was sure that Duane would too.

After a few months, I made a very calculated decision to lose my virginity. A close girlfriend told me, "if you want him to marry you, you will have to have sex first." I believed her because she was already married and pregnant with her first child. My yearning to know that Duane loved me, my deep desire to have him for my husband, overrode any fear that he would leave me after we had sex. I decided to take the risk. He kept right on standing me up now and then, and I couldn't always count on what he told me, but I believed that marriage would change him, that marriage was the magic answer.

After we began to double date with Duane's sister Devere and her fiancee Bill, the four of us began to talk about getting married at the same time. No specific proposal ever came from Duane; the idea of marriage just gradually materialized. I was not pregnant, so there was not that pressure, and I was grateful for that. We finally decided to drive to Angola, Indiana, a marriage mill town with no waiting period. We would be married in a double ceremony. My family couldn't afford to give me a church wedding, and Bill and DeVere didn't want one. In December 1950, a year and a half after my high school graduation, we arrived in Angola to discover that the legal age for men to be married there was twenty-one. I was eighteen, the legal age for women, but Duane was only twenty. Bill and DeVere decided to go ahead with their wedding. I spent most of the time in tears. However, two days later, Duane's parents drove back to Angola with us and signed permission papers for the marriage. I was finally Mrs. Roy Duane Keller. Surely, "happily ever after" was mine at last!

We moved into a small furnished apartment, and I continued to be employed by Michigan Bell. Duane was working on gas pipe line construction jobs with "good 'ol boys" who did a lot of after-hours drinking, and Spike (Duane's "good'ol boy" name) drank right along with them. Before the first week of marriage was over, Duane was not coming home in time for the evening meal. Sometimes it was ten or eleven in the evening; sometimes it was two or three in the morning. He always assured me that he was merely socializing with the boys, that he loved me and all was well. Very hurt, upset and angry, I cried night after night until there were no tears left to cry. My dream come true was rapidly disintegrating.

The continuing frustration of feeling abandoned triggered the temper that I left behind at age ten. I screamed and threw dishes, sobbed and threatened, but nothing changed. Before I could reach the conclusion that I would be better off by myself, I discovered that I was pregnant. In those years before birth control pills and legal abortion, it never occurred to me not to have the baby. Very sick the whole time, I left my job three months into the pregnancy and spent mornings in bed, afternoons on the sofa, and many evenings wringing my hands, pacing the floor and crying about my absent husband.

However, during the rare times when Duane was not drinking, I forgot about the periods of loneliness and rejection; I poured out my love to him and felt loved in return. During those times we visited our families, enjoyed movies and visited friends. We loved the Michigan lakes and the time we spent swimming and boating. We had a close relationship with Roy and Ollie, and I often stayed with them when Duane was out of town working the pipeline. Being with them helped relieve the misery of being separated from their son.

Relaxed and cozy in bed with Duane one Sunday morning just before the birth of our baby, I felt very loved and cherished as we talked about names. We both wanted a boy and finally decided on the name Richard. My favorite high school teacher had been Richard Blanchard who represented high aspirations and ideals to me and whose family seemed so warm and loving and together. I so very much wanted our baby to have a secure childhood and an opportunity to grow up normally. In those rare and precious moments, I had real hope that Duane would settle down and that my dreams of a happy marriage would be realized after all. Yet, even in this time of closeness, when the opportunity was there, I did not share my traumatic childhood with Duane because I had deliberately buried it in the back of my mind. I believed a happy marriage could make up for any past unhappiness. I had no conscious knowledge of the deep seated shame and pain that lurked just beneath the surface of my everyday awareness.

Richard's birth was long and difficult, but we were thrilled with our new baby boy. Unfortunately, this did not magically transform Duane into the ideal husband or father. The drinking continued, and my friends began to drop hints that he was being seen here and there with other women. When I confronted him, he insisted that he spent time with his men friends only. I believed this because I so very much wanted to.

The first painful and undeniable proof of his interest in other women came when Richard was nine months old. Duane came home early, ate supper, bathed, dressed, and left the house. I did not question him or try to convince him to stay home because I was ill with the flu and had no energy to argue. About an hour later, Gloria, a dear and close friend since grade school, phoned me. Her husband was in Korea in the service, so Gloria was a frequent visitor in our home and went out with us occasionally.

"Julie, Duane was just here at my house and asked me to go out with him," Gloria reported. I had a difficult time comprehending what she was saying. As long as I'd known Gloria, and good and trusted friend that she was, I still couldn't believe it! "What is he wearing?" I asked in total shock. She described exactly what he was wearing. Overwhelmed by information I couldn't deny, I decided that I needed to leave Duane. "It's quite obvious that he does not love me," I told myself. "I'll just have to figure out a way to get along without him." I packed up our things and "went home to mother." She was very understanding and welcoming. It was a few days before Easter. Two days later Duane showed up to talk to me. He was crying. He was sorry. "I promise to stop drinking," he entreated, his voice breaking. "Please give me another chance; I'll never do anything like that again." He had a stuffed

Easter toy for Richard. I couldn't resist. We went home together, and he stopped drinking for two weeks. Variations of this scene played out many times in the eleven years of our marriage. I would reach the limit of my endurance and leave. Duane would come after me, begging, crying, promising. I could never resist his tears. I kept hoping and praying that we might somehow work things out and begin to lead some kind of normal life without alcohol.

When Richard was a little over two years old and nothing had changed as far as Duane's drinking and frequent absence from home, I decided that I could no longer tolerate the resulting misery. I decided to leave, to go so far away that Duane wouldn't be able to work his persuasive powers on me. After he left for work early one September morning, I loaded our late model Mercury with all the belongings I could stuff into the car. Richard and I headed out for Sioux City, Iowa, where Gloria's husband was then stationed. I planned to stay with them and look for a job. I left a note that we were leaving and why, but I didn't reveal where we were going.

The trip was tiring and the weather unusually warm, but we arrived safely. After a rest, I left Richard with Gloria and went job hunting, but found nothing desirable. I was so distraught that it didn't occur to me to check with the telephone company about employment. I assumed that because I had worked for them less than a year in Michigan that they would not hire me in a new location. I didn't have enough confidence to even try anything besides restaurant work. I looked at the apartments that I could afford on a waitress' salary; they were dirty, dingy, and in poor neighborhoods. I couldn't bring myself to put Richard and myself in that situation if there was any alternative.

Jean, a close friend from high school, lived in Houston, Texas, and I had kept in contact with her and her husband, T.D. When I phoned and talked to them about what was happening, they invited us to come and stay with them. "There might be more job opportunities in Houston," they suggested. I realized that the hot and humid trip might be difficult for Richard, but desperate and determined to find a better life for us, I felt I had no choice but to go ahead with it anyway.

In spite of the fact that the car was not air conditioned, most of the trip went extremely well; however, one hot afternoon I lost control and slapped Richard because he spilled an orange soda on the car seat. I felt ashamed about this at the time, but put it out of my mind, my conscious mind that is. It was a relief for both of us to finally reach our destination. Jean and T.D. didn't have children, but wanted them very much and were happy to have Richard and I stay with them until I could get established. They treated us like family, and my heart will always be full of appreciation for these dear people. It was a joy to see Richard and T.D. playing and laughing together. "Perhaps we will break out of the alcohol filled life after all," I told myself.

But my period was late. I finally went to a doctor. Yes, I was pregnant. Jean and T.D. made it clear that Richard and I were welcome to stay with them and that I could have the baby there, but I felt it was too much to ask. I had no income, and I didn't believe I could count on Duane for help. I couldn't allow Jean and T.D. to support us for months, and then deal with a new baby besides. I didn't consider an illegal abortion. I had heard too many horror stories. If they had been safe and legal, I might have made a different decision. So, it seemed that the only alternative was to call Duane and tell him about my pregnancy.

He was happy to hear from me and relieved that Richard and I were safe. When I told him I was pregnant, he expressed his gratitude: "I've had this chance to think things over, and I'm going to change," he promised. "I'm going to stop drinking. I thank God for another chance to be with my family." A few days later, we picked him up at the Houston airport. He had arranged for time away from work so that he could drive us home. The trip back to Michigan was a happy reunion, a warm, close, and loving time. I believed. We enjoyed about two months of domestic peace; then the old pattern of drinking began again. This pregnancy was no easier than the first one. I was extremely tired, too tired to do anything but take care of Richard and the house, and to rest at every opportunity. I didn't have the energy to be angry.

Robert was born in 1954 and Colleen in 1958. Both were healthy, beautiful babies. Neither had been planned for; both were conceived while I was using a diaphragm, but I loved my children very much and wanted to give them the love and stability I missed growing up. Even though Duane drank and was away from home much of the time, his wages were high enough that we were well provided for. We owned a cottage on Lake George where we enjoyed much of the summer. I could afford to hire someone to help with housework and child care. Hoping that we would eventually lead a more normal life, I busied myself with the immediate task of taking care of the children. They were my joy and comfort, and I was dedicated to making their childhood better and happier than mine was. When hearing of tragic things happening to other people's children, I felt so very sorry for the parents and thought to myself, "The one thing I could never stand is something happening to my kids; I can't imagine how parents can endure such a thing." Unfortunately, I was about to find out.

One morning when Robert was two years old, I noticed he was running a fever. I called the doctor's office and made an appointment for that afternoon. Just as I was about to serve the boys their lunch, Robert's eyes rolled back in his head, he turned blue and started convulsing. I sent Richard to the neighbor for help while I ran water in the bathtub. Someone had told me that first hot and then cold water would bring a child out of a convulsion. The neighbor arrived, took one look and declared, "We'd better go to the emergency room." All the way there,

Robert was still convulsing. The doctors took a spinal tap and decided to send him by ambulance to the university hospital in Ann Arbor, nearly 200 miles south. Duane was working out of town, so his parents took care of Richard, and I rode with Robert in the ambulance. I could do nothing but cry and pray to God that he would survive. Later that evening, by the time Duane arrived with my mom, Robert's convulsions had stopped, but he remained unconscious and his fever was still climbing. It was uncertain if he would make it through the night; all we could do was continue to pray.

Miraculously, the next morning when Duane and I walked into his room, Robert opened his eyes, looked at me and said, "Hi, Mommy." He was okay! God answered our prayers, and Robert's life was spared, but we discovered later that he would grow up with serious problems. After we brought him home, he seemed fine for the next two years. Then, he began to have seizures. We took him back to the university hospital for complete tests and then follow-up every six months for several years. We were told a variety of things about what to expect in the future and about how he should be treated, - such opposite things as "he will outgrow the seizures and lead a normal life," and "there is nothing to be done; he'll end up in an institution." His medicine was adjusted and then readjusted. In spite of all that, his seizures continued, occasionally being so severe he had to be hospitalized for a day or two. I couldn't even consider for a moment the possibility that he would not be able to lead a normal life in the future.

All during these years, Duane continued to alternate between short periods of sobriety and longer times of heavy drinking. It amazed me that he could manage to hold a highly paid responsible position as a pipeline superintendent and still drink as much as he did. People seemed naturally drawn to him, and I wondered what he could achieve if he did not handicap himself with alcohol. The winter after Robert's first illness was a grace period for us; Duane stopped drinking. We took a long car trip to California with the boys. We wanted to escape the harsh Michigan winter and to enjoy new parts of the country. I had never traveled outside of a cold climate in wintertime before, and it was a thrill to see palm trees for the first time. Richard and Robert, excited about going to Disneyland, were behaving extremely well. Richard's sweet and loving nature came through in discussions about what he wanted to do to help people. He asked if we could send CARE packages to those people in need that he had seen on television.

We were invited to visit Duane's aunt and uncle and my dad's sister and her husband in southern California. Gracious and hospitable, these people opened their homes and hearts to us. Richard was delighted to see so many things he could share at "Show and Tell" when he returned to kindergarten. However, Richard did some telling on us soon after we arrived at the home of my aunt. It did not occur to us that he might be asking for help when he stated in a "show and tell" voice, "My daddy gets drunk, and my mommy gets mad and throws things at him." At that moment I wanted the floor to open up and swallow me. Embarrassed, I took him into the bedroom and chastised him for sharing private family matters in front of other people. But if our hosts were shocked or embarrassed, they didn't reveal it. They not only told us about Knott's Berry Farm, but insisted on taking us there in their car. The total trip was a great success and fun for us all.

Back home in Michigan, I began to go to church more often and to get serious in my bargaining sessions with God. Grateful that God answered my prayer that Robert would not die, I hoped that God would answer another one for me. "Dear Lord," I implored, "I will try harder to be a loving wife and perfect mother; PLEASE make Duane stop drinking so that he will be a good husband and father!" Because we had a close and loving family life when Duane was sober, the times of loneliness when he was absent or drunk seemed even more miserable because I knew it did not have to be that way. Yet, in spite of my desperate pleas, nothing changed for long, and I began to suspect that God was not going to help me. I began to wonder if He was really there at all, and if He was, I wanted to tell Him off. "God, I'm angry because I am doing the best I know how, and it looks like You don't care about us!"

Then, after I became pregnant with Colleen, Duane remained sober for months. Perhaps God was going to answer my prayers after all! Duane did not go out to the bars; we were close and enjoyed many family activities. It was our longest happy time together. In February, I gave birth to our own little girl, and I was ecstatic. It had finally come together. It was going to work out after all!

In the spring, Duane's pipeline work resumed, and with it his drinking began anew and intensified. Along with the emotional pain of this setback, I had continued problems with cramps and back pain. My doctor suggested that if my uterus was removed, the problems would be solved. I knew it would be better to not have more children, and I certainly wanted relief from my symptoms, so seven months after Colleen's birth, I went ahead with the surgery. I did indeed feel physically better and had more energy, but the emotional stress of Duane's increased drinking was extremely difficult to handle, and I become more and more embittered.

One night after the children were in bed asleep, Duane came home drunk and passed out on our bed. The accumulated frustrations, disappointments, and broken dreams of the past several years mocked me and pushed my emotions over the edge. "I can't take it anymore!" I screamed silently. The plastic bags that were over the dry cleaning in the closet and the warning on them about the danger of suffocation flashed into my mind. I walked to the closet and took one of these bags from the cleaning. I was going to put it over Duane's head because I knew we would be better off if he were dead. Detached and emotionless, I watched myself from a distant corner of the ceiling as my brain struggled with the problem of just exactly how to place the bag so he wouldn't regain consciousness and struggle. Then, a strong, stern, clear message, as clear as if someone were shouting in my ear: "Julie! Stop! If you do this, you will never be able to live with yourself, never forgive yourself!" These words brought me back to sanity. "Dear God, what have I almost done?" Cleansing tears began to stream down my face. Horrified, I knew that I must find a way to take charge of my own life, to get myself out of this impossible situation.

Determined to prepare to support myself and the children, I signed up for some correspondence courses - the Newspaper Institute of America writing course, Business English, and Stenotype, the machine short-hand that court reporters used. I was reinforced in this determination by reading <u>The Feminine Mystique</u> by Betty Friedan. This was the first that I began to understand that my happiness and well being did not have to totally depend on a man's presence in my life. The problem was I understood this only intellectually. Unfortunately, it would be several years before I would truly take charge of my own life, several years before I would have the opportunity to begin the transforming process of understanding and healing.

I did not allow the part of me that wanted to kill Duane to act out that impulse, but anger and bitterness were pushing to express, to find an avenue for revenge. I asked myself, "Why should I be faithful to such a disgusting drunk?" I answered myself, "He does just as he pleases; his boss, the guys that work under him, and any woman he wants to fool around with think he's just great. It's not fair. If that's the way the world works, then I will just do as I damn well please myself, - what does it matter!" I began to hire baby sitters and go out drinking and dancing myself. I knew several of the "good 'ol boys'" wives whose hus-bands were out of town working a great deal of the time, so we decided to go out together.

I met someone and had an affair. I resorted to this because I was bitter and angry and because a part of me was still searching for a "magic other" to fix my life. I was at the mercy of the strong unrecognized and unhealed emotions of my inner child who was desperate for love and validation. These emotions pushed me to prove I was still an attractive and desirable woman. I was unable to let go of the dream of a Prince Charming and happily ever after; I was unable to recognize Duane's behavior as the disease of alcoholism. I blamed him for making me miserable because I didn't know how to take responsibility for my own happiness. As far as I was concerned, he was the perpetrator and I the victim.

The relationship between Duane and me continued to deteriorate rapidly. He drank more and more. I became increasingly bitter and angry and acted out my frustration in ways that could only be destructive to me and to the children. Something had to change; I decided it was time to separate from Duane again. After finding a secretarial job, I asked him to move out. A reliable neighbor, an older woman, cared for two year old Colleen during the day while I worked. The boys were now both in school. It was January. Although Duane begged for another chance, I had lost all trust; my heart closed to him, and I refused.

In March, Duane checked himself into a detox hospital and joined Alcoholics Anonymous. Again, he asked to reconcile, but I resisted. Then, the doctor from the program called me to plead Duane's case. Unable to resist the persuasion of an authority figure, I relented. "OK, one more time!" However, I determined to keep a secret internal defense system. Hurt and disappointed too many times already, I was skeptical about Duane's ultimate recovery. A part of me remained inside a protective wall, cold and uncaring, so I wouldn't be devastated if Duane returned to drinking.

In May, I left my secretarial job in order to be with the children and enjoy the summer with them at our lake cottage. I planned special birthday parties for both boys. Richard was especially appreciative and spent some of his birthday money to buy a decorative cup for me as a thank you. We purchased a new three bedroom home a short distance from the elementary school and made arrangements to move in August. Duane and I attended meetings of AA and Al-Anon. Everything was going extremely well. Yet, I remained walled off inside, waiting to see if it was safe to trust.

We met Wayne and Joanne through AA, became friends and decided to spend a vacation together. Duane's boss owned a cabin in Canada at Lake-in-the-Woods and made it available to us for a week. Wayne and Joanne had a son Casey, a little older than our Richard. We took Richard and Casey along with us and left Robert and Colleen with Roy and Ollie. On the drive through upper Michigan en route to Canada we enjoyed Fort Mackinaw, the Mackinaw Bridge, and all the tourist attractions. Once at the cabin, we were very impressed with the pristine beauty of the lakes and dreamed about buying a piece of property in that location. Sightseeing, fellowship, fishing - we had wonderful fun in a magical setting with perfect summer weather. The beginning of a healing? A little hope began to filter through my defensive wall.

About two days before we were to start home, Richard developed flu-like symptoms. I gave him aspirin and made sure that he rested quietly. At first, he seemed to be doing okay, but the next day his fever was higher. We decided to take him to a doctor in nearby Kenora, where he was given antibiotics. It was treated as a routine case. In spite of this, I felt uneasy. We decided to begin our journey home a day early. Richard seemed a little better as we began the drive home and ate a small evening meal in the restaurant when we stopped for the night.

It was a peaceful Sunday morning with little traffic, and Richard was resting his head on my lap as we drove along. "I'm not going to fight with Robert anymore, and when we get home I'm going to give him this quarter," he told me, seeming anxious to get home too. A few minutes later, he began to cough and choke. At the nearest emergency room, the examining doctor informed us that he believed Richard had polio. I couldn't believe that! He'd had immunization shots. "We must get him as soon as possible to Marquette, where all polio patients in the Upper Peninsula are sent," the doctor urged. "I'll order an ambulance right away." Riding with Richard while Duane and the others followed in the car, I tried to reassure him, "You're going to be fine." His eyes met mine as he answered, "You hope so, Mom - you hope so."

At the hospital in Marquette, Richard was immediately given a tracheotomy to aid his breathing. The doctor took Duane and I aside and cautioned us, "he might die." Inside my head, I shouted at God: "I have been through so much already - don't you DARE take Richard's life!" I simply refused to believe that Richard was in danger of dying - the possibility was too horrible to accept. I set up a dialogue with myself: "Maybe he will be very sick, maybe even for a long time, but he has to get well!" In a mutual state of denial, Duane and I informed our friends that we would be staying in Marquette with Richard until he was well enough to travel. We didn't share the doctor's warning with them because we couldn't accept its validity.

"You take the car on home," we urged them. "We'll get a room within walking distance of the hospital and worry about getting home later." By the time our friends were on their way, it was late afternoon. We checked back in with Richard and his special duty nurse. "Think about something special you'd really like, even a pony, and when you're better you can have it," I said to Richard in a desperate attempt to encourage him in his obvious struggle. He could only nod his head and look at me with eyes filled with pain. After she gave him pain medication, the nurse assured us that Richard would rest and suggested we walk down the street and rent our room before it got any later. "Richard, we love you. We are going to rent a room, but we'll be back soon to sit with you. We'll be right here with you until you're better." In the room we began to unpack our things, planning to wash up a little and get right back to the hospital. I heard a phone ring in the hall. The woman we were renting from answered it. Sensing that it was for us, I opened the door and listened. "Yes, I'll tell them," she said.

"You're wanted back at the hospital right away," she informed me. When we walked through the big doors into the main lobby, the doctor was waiting for us. I knew by the expression on his face what he was going to tell us. "No! It can't be! It's not true - Please - it's not true!" But it was true. I cried out and shook my head, but I couldn't stop it from being true. "Your son is gone," the doctor said quietly. We were immediately escorted to a separate room and given tranquilizers. We were not allowed to cause a disturbance.

There was no family, no friends. Just the two of us and that awful heavy numbness. A nightmare beyond belief. Those around us instructed us to do certain things: "Buy some dress clothes for him to be laid out in." "Go to the funeral home, talk to the director; pick out a casket." "Make arrangements to transport yourselves and Richard's body home." We desperately wanted to return home as soon as possible, but we could not stand the thought of leaving Richard behind, so we arranged for the funeral director to prepare Richard's body and then drive us in the hearse the 500 miles home.

In miserable silence, because we knew there were no words we could utter that would bring comfort, Duane and I hung on to each other's hand and endured the ride home. I was sure God was punishing me for my defiant attitude and other sins by taking Richard from us. My chest felt so heavy that the only way I could manage to take each breath was to repeat the Lord's Prayer over and over again to myself. I felt I deserved punishment, and asked God for help and mercy. I felt especially anguished because we were not with Richard when he died.

My tortured thoughts went around and around: "Perhaps he would still be alive if we had stayed in the room. Why didn't just one of us leave to rent our room? How could I have left him, even for a minute? It might be my fault he's dead. Oh God, it hurts!" It was too much effort to breathe; the muscles in my chest couldn't deal with what felt like a hundred pound weight. I forced my mind back to the Lord's Prayer and somehow managed to breathe, one anguished breath at a time.

Finally home, family and friends surrounded us. A part of me wanted to scream and cry and carry on, but I didn't know how to give myself permission to do it. Yes, I cried quietly, but mostly when I was alone or just with Duane. We stumbled through the visiting time at the funeral home and the funeral itself in a heavy hearted daze, although we derived comfort from the outpouring of support from friends and neighbors. A couple who lost their own child came to support us and to tell us that although it was difficult to believe, the pain would slowly diminish. Before the casket was closed for the last time, I leaned into it and began to sob. Someone immediately took me by the arm and led me away. No public hysterics were allowed here either. I began to realize that I must find a way to deal with my grief in private.

Moving day arrived a few days after the funeral. Richard had been looking forward to living in this new three bedroom ranch home with room in the basement for him to work with wood and his other little boy projects. Now, I would gladly have blown up the house and all material possessions if only we could have Richard back - but we could not. So, we moved into our new home, but there was no joy in it, only the pain of knowing our son would not be there to share it with us. We were expected to get on with our normal lives, but normal no longer existed. I could not step out on the porch and call Richard from his play to come in the house for dinner. The evening meal was agony because Richard was not in his place at the table. When I awoke in the morning, there was just a second or two when I could believe Richard was still with us, that the past days were only a nightmare. But then the reality hit: "It's true. He's dead." The hundred pound weight continued to press down upon my heart.

As the first agonizing weeks dragged by, I continually felt weak, dizzy, and nauseated. Unable to determine what was wrong with me, my doctor sent me to the hospital for tests. The diagnosis: over breathing due to stress and grief. "Breathe into a paper bag when attacks of nausea and dizziness strike," the doctors instructed. "You are basically in good health." The first morning after that diagnosis, just before I awoke, I had a vivid dream of Richard's presence that remained very clear even after I awakened. He had a definite message for me: "Mom! I'm alright! I love you all. Take care of my brother and sister." It was very comforting to hear these positive words from Richard, and I realized he was right. I needed to stop being selfish. I needed to keep going and make a life for the children who were still here and who needed me.

I attempted to find productive activities that would give me enough energy to share with Colleen and Robert. I wanted to give them the attention they deserved and felt Richard was somehow watching over that effort. I continued to work on my correspondence courses and added a new activity. I began to sell jewelry and clothing on the home party plan. Working with the attractive quality costume jewelry, the colorful sporty clothing and the women who sought my advice about them was therapeutic. Bookings were scheduled so I could have plenty of time with the children. I was doing better, but I certainly had not dealt with my guilt and grief. I merely buried it in that overflowing chest with all my other unresolved issues.

When Duane began drinking again, I was not surprised. If drinking could have eased my own pain, and if I had not been responsible for Colleen and Robert, I probably would have knocked myself out with booze too. One Saturday night, about six months after Richard's death, I was home alone with the children. I knew that Duane was out drinking, but I no longer allowed myself to get upset about his activities. I was just trying to survive from day to day. I read until 2:00 am., turned out the light and went to sleep. I awakened because Duane was shaking my shoulder. "Wake up! There's someone I want you to meet." I assumed he was referring to one of his drunken buddies, so I told him, "Go away, I don't feel like getting up to make breakfast for you." However, he kept insisting and wouldn't leave me alone. Finally, I got out of bed, threw on an old purple chenille robe and staggered out into the kitchen with one eye open.

Once there, both eyes popped open. I was shocked wide awake. A very pregnant woman was standing by the kitchen door. In a split second I knew the whole story, but I kept silent. A part of me was present in the room, but another part of me was distanced and detached, watching this drama like it was a scene in a movie starring someone else. I waited for someone to speak. "This is Phyllis - she's pregnant, and I'm the father," he informed me. "I guess we need a divorce." I made coffee and we all sat and drank it, talking calmly, like we were discussing the weather. Watching this scene from the ceiling, I saw that Duane and I had come to the final act of our play. "You can have him," I said to Phyllis. I'm sick of this whole ugly drunken life. You can have him and good riddance." They left together. We were in agreement about a divorce.

The next morning at eleven o'clock, Duane, obviously still drinking heavily, appeared at the back door. He was alone. He wanted to talk more about the situation. "I still love you," he slurred. In this moment I lost control. I was standing near a kitchen drawer, and I pulled it open, grabbed a knife, and screamed, "get out of here!" After Duane left, I began to regret that he was not sober, that we didn't talk.

Years later I discovered that a high percentage of parents divorce the first year after a child's death; they mirror too much pain for each other. Would Duane have remained sober if Richard had not died? Would we have been able to save our marriage under sober circumstances? I can only wonder. That spring our divorce was final and Duane married Phyllis. With a six year old handicapped son and a three year old daughter to support, I needed to find work. Duane was paying child support, but it did not provide enough for us to live comfortably. With only a high school education, I knew I would be challenged. However, in spite of being engulfed in a huge ball of pain and uncertainty, I discovered a pocket of courage that propelled me forward. I was determined to re-discover the higher vision of life I had buried with bitterness and disillusionment, for Colleen and Robert's sake as well as for my own. At twenty-nine years old, I felt like an old woman, but I was determined to be a survivor, to regain my faith in life. A phrase that had helped me through past rough times comforted me once more: "I am hurt, but I am not slain; I'll lay me down and bleed awhile, then I'll rise and fight again."

CHAPTER FOUR
ANOTHER RUN AT LIFE

We're all children, even the wisest of us.
We're all five year olds learning to do
this thing called life.
-Byron Katie

My lawyer, who needed someone to fill in part time, offered me a job, and I was grateful, but I needed to look around for something permanent. Luckily, while at the post office one afternoon, I ran into the government quality control supervisor at the manufacturing plant in town. He was a friendly older man I had often chatted with when I worked in the plant, and when I told him about my situation, he said, "My secretary is leaving, and we need someone for our office - would you be interested?" I certainly was! He was able to hire me as a temporary employee until I could take a civil service test.

On the day of the test, which was given in a city over 100 miles away, the roads were a glare of ice from freezing rain. Determined to not let anything stop me from getting the job, I left home early and drove slowly and carefully, managing to arrive at the test site safely and on time. In spite of nerves from the precarious trip and anxiety about the test, I passed it and settled into secure employment with the federal government. The salary for a clerk-stenographer was not outstanding, but higher than most secretarial positions, and it came with benefits. On the home front, an ad for an older woman to live with us and help with the children had produced good results. Mrs. Fairchild became a part of our household and did a good job with the children for a very reasonable salary.

In spite of the fact that things seemed to be coming together, and in spite of my initial courage and determination, I had periods of feeling totally helpless and endangered, as if ravening wolves were circling, ready to pounce and devour me at any moment. I felt a tremendous need to find a new man, a man who would marry me and take care of us. Although part of me felt better off without Duane, another part regretted the divorce. Full of fear and in a state of vacillation between blaming myself and blaming Duane, words from a self-help book provided some clarity and a degree of peace: "The first step toward inner peace is to stop blaming others and to begin to see our own blame, but the process is not complete until we blame no one." During one of Duane's visits to the children, I asked to speak with him alone for a few minutes. "I'm really sorry for any pain I've caused you," I said. "I'm sorry it didn't work out for us." And Duane answered, "I'm sorry too," However, we both knew that it was impossible to unscramble eggs, too late to go back and do things another way.

Mom and my brothers were supportive, but other concerns were more important right then. My brother Wilbur and his wife Virginia had five young children, and Wilbur had been supporting them with his job as a tree trimmer. After dealing for ten days with a sore throat that wouldn't go away, he finally went to a doctor and was informed that he had a fast growing incurable cancer. The cancer took only two months to kill him; he was thirty-two. He had not worried about taking out life insurance at such a young age, so Virginia was forced to raise the children on what she received from social security. My divorce problems seemed small compared to what Virginia was faced with.

Although Wilbur and Virginia had a simple lifestyle and no extra material possessions, they loved each other and their children very much.

At the time, I couldn't help but wonder why people who are happy to-gether so often become torn apart by the death of one of them. My dear friend Barbara and her husband Gene were so happy and in love when she died right after the birth of their child. It seemed that love and in-credible pain too often went hand in hand. I had not yet been blessed with an understanding about soul choice and Earth School lessons.

Soon after the divorce, I found that as a woman alone; I had more opportunities for male company than I wanted. Several men made it apparent to me that they were willing to provide limited "companion-ship." I was shocked when a married acquaintance stopped by to ex-press sympathy for my situation and offered to "take care of me in bed." No wonder I had fears about hungry wolves! Yet, I was not deterred from wanting a good husband, a Prince Charming who would take of me and the children.

Because Mrs. Fairchild was home in the evenings, I felt free to occa-sionally go to bars with women friends who were also looking for the right and perfect mate. That there were healthier places to look for male companionship didn't occur to us. On one of our bar excursions, a handsome blonde, blue eyed young man asked me to dance. Something about him reminded me of my high school first love. I appreciated his carefree and happy disposition, and we began to date. Although Ted (not his real name) was five years younger than me and had never been married, he soon assured me that he wanted to settle down. We felt a mighty physical attraction for each other, and the whirlwind romance began. Ted and the children liked each other and got along well, and I saw that he would be kind to them. He was steadily employed by the state of Michigan as an equipment operator for the highway de-partment. When he proposed, promising to never treat me like Duane did, I breathed a sigh of relief and counted my blessings because I had found such a stable person to share my life. It took me less than six months after the divorce to find a new husband.

During the first weeks of our marriage, I began to realize that Ted was not truly interested in companionship after all. I felt like a prize that, once won, could be put on the shelf and ignored, except for sex of course. Ted spent a great deal of his time at home napping. When awake, he was restless. Often, he left the house immediately after the evening meal and went down to the bar to play cards and talk to his buddies.

Still living at home when we met, Ted was the kind of guy whose mother had always taken very good care of him. The closest he ever came to fixing himself something to eat was to reach into the refrigerator and pull out a cold hot dog. His clothes dropped to the floor, and I was expected to pick them up. I never had these issues with Duane, who was neat and picked up after himself, who even enjoyed cooking when he was home and not drinking. It was becoming obvious to me that the most satisfying thing about this marriage to Ted was the sex. The problem was that the other twenty-three hours in the day weren't that great. Too often I felt like I'd taken on another child. I wanted to be taken care of by Ted, but he expected to be taken care of by me. He didn't seem to understand that by spending so much time down at the tavern, he was doing just what Duane had done and what he had promised he would never do.

Thus, the old pattern began to repeat itself with a new partner. I decided to stay with Ted, hoping that his behavior would change. After a few months of this, I realized that change was not likely, so I decided to leave him. I knew that I couldn't keep up the house payments for long with my income alone, so I allowed the house to go back to the people who were holding the contract. The furniture made a down payment on a mobile home, and we moved to a park closer to my work. Very ignorant about what I probably should have received from Duane for child support, I was grateful that his modest check was regular and on time, and I just accepted what it was. I also had a desire to make it on my own and not give Duane and Phyllis the satisfaction of needing to provide extra help.

During our separation, Ted and I agreed that we were free to see other people, and I did. However, it wasn't long before Ted asked me out to dinner and asked to take the children on outings. Ted's approach was a bit different from Duane's. Ted did not cry; he simply turned on the sincere charm. When we were separated, the courting dance began all over, and I became the center of his world. He seemed fascinated by me, and couldn't spend enough time with me and the children. This convinced me that he had changed and that he would surely continue this family focused behavior once we were living together again.

However, once back in the role of live-in husband, something clicked off. Ted was not interested in the ongoing routine of marriage and soon returned to the after work pattern of sleeping or spending hours in the bars. After a time of this, I decided on another separation, and the whole pattern repeated itself. This scenario played itself out several times during the nine years we were married.

During one of these separations, I was introduced to an eligible wealthy older bachelor who took a great liking to me and the children. He invited us to spend time at his beautiful country home, and introduced us to his friends. Bill wanted me to divorce Ted so that we could be married. I was inclined to do this, so we continued to date and think about being together permanently. However, I soon began to realize that although I was very fond of Bill and enjoyed spending time with him, I was not "in love" with him. "It would not be fair to you for us to marry," I confessed, and he accepted this graciously.

Before long, Ted began to court me again, and I was drawn back into the old circumstances. It would be years before I came to see and to understand my emotions and motivations: I didn't know how to be "in love" with an emotionally mature man who treated me well, even though I consciously very much wanted this. The unconscious need to transform a problem husband into a perfect Prince Charming caused me to repeatedly make unwise choices concerning the men in my life.

After the first three years of marriage, which were interspersed with periodic separations, a better way of life presented itself. My brother Will worked in an office at the same plant where I was employed by the government, and he often stopped by say hello. When I had spare time, I gladly typed some of his class papers. He was close to getting his degree after several years of attending college nights and weekends. What he was doing sounded very interesting and satisfying to me, but I didn't believe myself capable of doing such a thing.

"I've been out of school too long," I lamented. "I'm not sure that I'm smart enough to go back and do the studying now. Besides, I'd never be able to handle the math and science requirements because I did poorly in those high school subjects." Will assured me there would be no problem; I could always get tutoring if I needed it. "Why not just try a few classes," he suggested. With his encouragement, I studied some old math books and arranged to take the SAT test. To my surprise, I scored high in everything except math and science and was admitted into Central Michigan University in Mt. Pleasant, where I began with two Saturday classes, Speech and English.

The atmosphere of school was so stimulating for me, and I performed so well in those first classes that I knew I wanted to finish, no matter what. The first day I walked onto the campus in February of 1965, I was very timid. This was the wild sixties. I felt like an old women in the midst of all the hippies, even though I was only thirty-two years old. Yet, the classes were fascinating; everyone was quite friendly, and I did not get eaten alive. I began to make friends with classmates and to experience a mutual respect between myself and the professors. Gradually taking on more student characteristics, I left my handbag at home and carried what I needed inside my notebook, imitating other young women students. I was able to leave my fear of the campus behind and rediscover the confidence that helped me achieve success in high school.

With Ted's blessing, I left the secretarial job and became a full time student. The three year retirement fund that had built up helped with tuition. Also, there was a teacher shortage, and the government was generous with loans for future teachers. I had decided to become a high school speech teacher. We moved just outside Ted's home town, a village of 500 people comprised of two taverns, two gas stations, a general store and a hardware. Ted's father, when he wasn't working or involved with the family hobby of harness horse racing, was a frequent customer at the taverns which seemed to be the primary social centers for the men of the town. Ted's parents did not have many mutual interests or spend much time together; I saw that they did not provide an example of companionship between husband and wife. However, I liked them both and enjoyed a good relationship with them. I was relieved when Colleen and Robert made friends and adapted well to their new school. We all felt good about the changes we were making.

Moving into a full time class schedule was exhilarating. Classes in psychology and sociology proved to be especially helpful because they provided some understanding of my own life. The objective viewpoints were comforting and helped me to see that picture book lives are not the norm for most people. So often in a survival mode, I felt that everyone else had a firmer grip on life, a basic happiness that I didn't have. Now I saw that my inner turmoil was possibly a natural consequence of difficult experiences. I saw that it might be possible to understand and to overcome those difficulties and maybe lead a basically normal and satisfying life.

The direction toward teaching high school speech was changed when a counselor assured me that English teachers could always find employment. Deciding to go for that security was easy because I loved reading and literature as much as I loved speech and drama. After the A's began to accumulate, I was invited to become an honor student with the privilege of several classes of independent study. The Shakespeare teacher encouraged me to continue on for a Master's degree and to go into college teaching. I was delighted to be encouraged to do that, but I certainly did not have the confidence to come up with the idea on my own.

Professors were friendly, and I was honored and surprised to be invited to their homes and parties. Although I enjoyed and appreciated this, a part of me felt like I didn't truly belong. I thought, "These people don't know about my crazy past, or see my mixed up insides. I'm sure if they really knew me, they'd never accept me." I was ashamed of the divorce from Duane and the separations and shaky relationship with my drinking blue collar husband. Yet, Ted and I tried to put some things together.

He enrolled in two classes and made good grades, but it was clear that this was not really his area of interest. His hobby was racing harness horses, the kind of race where the driver is pulled in a sulky behind the horse. His family had done this for years, mostly at county fairs. When we could, Robert, Colleen and I went along with Ted to these races and often helped shovel horse manure. We walked the horses to cool them out and cheered for Ted during the race. However, even during these outings, Ted was usually off talking to his buddies, not spending much time with us. I believe he sincerely loved us but was into a rut and was happy in it. As far as I knew, he was not interested in other women, and he was always good natured and kind to the children. That he was not interested in real relationship or companionship except with the boys at the bar was a continual frustration for me.

I focused my time and attention on doing well in school and taking care of Robert and Colleen's needs, living for the day that I would be self-supporting in a stimulating and challenging college atmosphere. Inspired by the examples of Emerson and Thoreau, I began a journal:

(first entry) 13 March 1967 Journals are no doubt old-fashioned these days, but inasmuch as I have a very old idea that I would like to someday be at least a competent writer - I'm willing to take any reasonable suggestion for accomplishing this. Emerson and Thoreau benefitted from the practice, and I'm studying them, so I'll take their suggestion. I feel that I have much in common with Emerson - mainly because he was an optimist to the point of foolishness - also because he lost his much loved son at age seven. His feelings of loss parallel mine after Richard died - also his later feelings of "buck up," which I understand because one either makes adjustments to grief or refuses to go on living.

14 April 1967 Journal: It seems that I am troubled with the chronic disease of dissatisfaction and a vague uneasiness about life. I feel there is something I should be doing, or something I am missing, but I don't know quite what. When I think of all those who have lived and died in utter frustration and despair, I wonder why I should be privileged over them. When I compare myself to those less fortunate, it puts down the uneasiness, at least for awhile. Perhaps I would feel better if I stopped procrastinating about writing - I would feel as though I were doing something constructive - even if it turns out rotten, which at first it no doubt would. Maybe I can get the same satisfaction out of writing that many people get out of travel, golf, bridge, drink-

ing or sex. Not that I couldn't appreciate some of each, but I'm beginning to see that real fulfillment in life probably cannot be found from these activities.

In the midst of continued study, self-examination, and pushing to learn more, do more, be more, the world again fell apart. After Robert began junior high, the pressures began to accumulate for him. Suddenly, he had many teachers, not just one that I could run interference with. He became more and more hyperactive and hostile in school and at home. The school psychiatrist called and informed me that Robert would no longer be allowed to attend school because of his violent behavior. I had no understanding about what the school or state's responsibility might have been in educating Robert. I did not question their authority. I took him out of school and then to the mental health clinic for several sessions.

At thirteen, Robert was very strong and nearly six feet tall. There was no question of disciplining him physically, and as he became more and more angry with me each day, I found myself becoming frightened of him. His tolerance for Colleen was also getting less and less, and I was afraid for her as well. Each day when I walked in the door from class, he would snarl, "What are YOU doing home? Why don't you just stay away?" He occupied himself by wadding up paper into hundreds of tiny little balls and throwing them around the room and at me. At night he wandered around the house unable to sleep, and I was afraid to sleep when he was not asleep. I realized that we needed help very badly; yet, we were not getting much of it at the clinic.

During this time Ted immersed himself in his usual interests. I begged him to help me, to talk to me about Robert's situation, to share his ideas about it with me, but he wasn't able or willing to do this. He stayed away from home even more than usual, and I was becoming more and more desperate. Duane was involved in his life with Phyllis, unwilling or unable to be responsible for helping with Robert. The psychologists at the mental health clinic were divided in their ideas, so they refrained from making any specific suggestions concerning what to do to help Robert. I was living on the edge of breakdown and collapse myself.

Finally, it was suggested that, at least temporarily, Robert be placed in a private or public institution. However, I would have to be the one to make the decision. Without any advice or support from Duane or Ted, I was on my own and tormented by the pressure of deciding what to do. The money was just not there for a private place for Robert. The idea of placing him in a public institution was terrifying. Yet, it was coming down to doing that because I feared for our safety I didn't know how much longer I could continue to live like this, but I was unable to decide what to do.

Going along day to day with little sleep, still attending classes and doing household chores and homework, I continued to deal with Robert as best I could but knew that I was close to breaking down. One evening, feeling totally at the end of my rope, I begged Ted to help me, to talk to me, to try to help me deal with Robert. Ted refused to even sit down and discuss these things. Suddenly, I lost all control. I screamed and grabbed books from the bookcase and threw them around the room - I was going totally berserk - I couldn't take it anymore!

Ted managed to calm me down and then helped restore the room to order. The next morning I called the clinic and arranged for Robert to be taken to the state hospital at Traverse City for evaluation. It would be determined there what could be done for him. The next day, Ted, Robert and I drove to the hospital in Traverse City. The psychiatrist there informed us that Robert would be tested and instructed us to check back with them in about a week. Leaving Robert in that hospital was pure hell for all of us. My heart was nearly as heavy as it had been when Duane and I rode 500 miles in a hearse with Richard's body in the back. In spite of the nightmare, I knew that I must remember Colleen and her needs. I knew I needed to somehow finish school. I clung to the hope that Robert would be helped. I had to believe in a better future because if I couldn't, I was afraid I'd give in to depression and kill myself.

The Traverse City state hospital became Robert's home for six years. At first, he was enrolled in their new model school, but he became violent and unruly enough that he was pulled out of it. A poem by Emily Dickinson became very meaningful to me because it described the pain around what had happened to my two sons:

> My life closed twice before its close.
> It yet remains to see
> if eternity reveal a third event to me.
> So huge, so hopeless to conceive as those that twice befell.
> Parting is all I know of Heaven and all I need of Hell."

One morning after a psychology class, I talked to the professor about my pain over Robert's problems. He suggested that I begin counseling with him, and after a few sessions, I joined his therapy group. It felt so good to be supported, and it was a revelation to me to discover that even young students had serious and painful problems of their own. I could support them too. I began to feel less alone and developed an even deeper interest in psychology and the help I felt it could offer people. As an English major, I was naturally exposed to great writers and their philosophies, which helped me to view life and my problems in a broader context. Over the years I had developed a certain philosophy of my own, which in spite of everything had been an optimistic view. Always searching for a way to escape my own pain and for a key that would unlock the door to the good life, I knew I wanted peace of mind, self-fulfillment, and of course, a loving partner.

Reading Emerson, Thoreau, Melville, Hawthorne, Shakespeare, Thomas Hardy and other greats and comparing their ideas about life and people helped bring my own philosophy into sharper focus. In some ways I could identify with Hardy's dark and pessimistic view. His main characters are victims of life's cruel circumstances. He sees God as swatting humans for sport, just as we might swat flies. However, I responded to Emerson's ideas and writing with a knowing that "this is truth for me." His optimism and faith in the ability of individuals to overcome and his cosmic view thrilled and inspired me. He talks about not being intimidated by "the hobgoblins of foolish consistency." Inconsistent and exploring as I'd been, that statement was a validation for me. He also said "be an opener of doors for such as come after thee, and do not make the universe a blind alley," - an inspiring suggestion for a teacher.

In spite of the positive and inspirational influence of school, there were days that the heartbreak over Robert threatened my will and strength to overcome. I wrote in my journal in August: "I am hurt but I am not slain - I'll lay me down and bleed awhile - then I'll rise and fight again." I want to live by this philosophy, but I'm not so sure I have any fight left. Today has been an extremely bad day. We traveled to the hospital yesterday expecting to take Robert out swimming. But he had changed buildings and doctors and no permission had been given. He is with children ages nine through seventeen and was supposed to be starting school today, but that's not happening because he is having a difficult time adjusting to his new situation. While I was talking to the attendant, a rat ran through the office. The paint is chipped off the walls; everything seems so dismal and dreary. Richard has been gone seven years now - if Robert has to be so miserable it would be better if he were with Richard. If I didn't have Colleen and Robert to care about, I'd feel like putting myself away.

After I bled awhile, I somehow managed to rise up and go on with my life's program. Fortunately, my busy schedule didn't include time to feel sorry for myself for long because every other weekend I traveled the 150 miles to Traverse City to visit Robert. Colleen often came along, but sometimes she stayed with a friend or with her father and Phyllis for the weekend. Ted sometimes came along, but not regularly. The visits were very depressing, but I found some emotional outlet by journaling:

> Monday January 15, 1968: I have been depressed and came home at ten this morning after two classes and cried and cried some more over Robert. This afternoon I called my psychology professor and walked up to talk with him and cried some more when I got there. He held my hand and told me I wasn't all alone in my suffering, and I felt less alone. Yet, I think in a way everyone IS alone. I suppose I'll have more days like this one - I just hope I can get through them without cracking or killing myself. It would be a relief to be out of my misery - especially on a day like this. I hope to God that Robert will eventually get better and that I didn't say the wrong thing to him yesterday. The pain I feel today seems to be pure pain. It is easier to feel guilty and believe that you thus deserve the pain. - Somehow it seems easier to bear. Thanks to counseling, I no longer feel as guilty, but the plain pain is still horrible. Yet, people who care make it easier to bear than it would be otherwise.

> Journal 5 Feb 1968: Today I feel completely demoralized. I don't feel pain. I feel as if a huge weight is slowly pressing my spirit for living - down, down, down. I would like to go to bed and never get up. -- I was

just interrupted by the ringing telephone. Brother Will is coming over for lunch. So I won't go under today. Maybe I'll have to start living from day to day like an alcoholic. If only the horrible God-awful tortures about Robert would stop. It seems they go on and on.

In the midst of this pain and frustration, I was saved by the challenge and fascination of learning. When I was studying or in class, life called to me, "Look at this - life does have something to offer - others have suffered, endured, overcome come on Julie, you can do it!" I graduated with a liberal arts degree in June of 1968, with a 3.87 grade point average. I placed second in my class of 1100. For an "old woman" afraid I'd have trouble keeping up with the young students, expecting I'd have to work hard to get C's, I was totally amazed, but proud of myself. I felt I had proved to myself and others that I was worthwhile, that I had something to offer.

I attended summer school and started work on a master's degree. In the fall, I began teaching two freshmen English classes as part of a graduate assistant program. The first day in front of the class, my hands and knees shook as I wrote the requirements for the class on the board. Looking at the list of students, I noticed that the son of one of the supervisors at the manufacturing plant where I had worked was in the class. I felt even more on the spot, yet proud too. My teaching career had begun!

Two other older female graduate assistants shared the office with me, and we became lifetime friends. We breezed through the year, and in June of 1969, Master's degree in hand, I began to job hunt. I had dreamed of going to a faraway romantic place like California, but I needed to stay close to Traverse City, where I could visit Robert and bring him home to visit regularly. Out of seven applications, I was invited to three interviews and was offered positions at two area colleges.

I chose Ferris State College in Big Rapids, Michigan because it had a growing student body of 10,000 and an atmosphere much like my alma mater, Central Michigan University. It was within commuting distance and only 100 miles from Traverse City.

The first year at Ferris, I commuted the fifty miles to Big Rapids. Ted's habits of absence from home did not change, and I could clearly see that I had a choice of living with that or leaving. I could now support myself, and I felt that I wanted to spend my time in more productive ways than driving 100 miles each day in order to be home to cook dinner for a husband who spent every evening in the bar. Even on the occasions that we did have an evening out together, we had trouble finding enough to talk about. When we were with his brothers or friends, the conversation revolved around horses and village gossip. I realized that I wanted more out of life than a dreary existence with someone whose goals and aspirations were so totally different from mine.

Yet, I went along from day to day, hoping that things would eventually be different. Then, I had an unusually clear and vivid dream that I remembered in great detail the next morning. It seemed to be urging me to move forward:

> I am down by the water's edge; it is night and foggy. A ship comes in close to shore and shines a light on me and wants to rescue me. I want to be rescued, but it is foggy, and I'm afraid to go out into the dark water. I just stand on shore and wait to be rescued. The ship waits and lowers a chain. I can see the light though the fog, and I feel a tremendous yearning to go out to it, but something seems to hold me back. The next morning the waters have receded. There is a chain on the sand where the ship had been, and the word SILLY is written in big letters in the sand. I'm sorry that I didn't

have the courage to go out and grab the chain and get
onto the lighted ship when I had the chance. I think,
"what good to gain the world and lose my own soul?"

The lighted ship seemed to symbolize my desire for a new, higher, and more satisfying existence. My psyche was telling me that I needed to move through the fog (the unknown), through the dark waters (my fearful emotions) and grab onto the chain (strength) that was being offered. It would be silly to "miss the boat" and be left stranded on the shore. My soul knew that it was useless to gain the world and not take care of my own soul growth.

As a result of this dream experience, I knew that I could not allow myself to be left stranded in a shallow mundane existence. I would somehow claim and utilize enough strength to move onto a forward path. I made up my mind that when school was out - I did not want Colleen to change schools in the middle of the year - we would move to Big Rapids and that I would divorce Ted. I knew that this would not be just another separation, another courting dance, and another reconciliation leading back to the same dead end routine. I knew, without a doubt, that it was time to stand firm and move forward into a new life.

CHAPTER FIVE
CONTINUING SEARCH FOR LOVE
AND TRUTH

"It is possible to see everything in a new light.
Where we see one thing at our level,
at a higher level, a million things exist. "
Maurice Nicoll

Although Ted felt some pain and tried to convince me not to divorce him, he did not make it a miserable situation, and the move to Big Rapids proceeded smoothly. We wanted to remain friends, and he came to Big Rapids several times to take Colleen and me out to dinner. When he raced his horse at the county fair in Big Rapids, Colleen and I watched the race and talked to him afterwards. However, the attachment had definitely been broken. I felt no animosity toward Ted and wished him the very best, while being absolutely certain that I could no longer be married to him. For several months, we continued to see each other occasionally just to talk, and Ted finally realized that a couple relationship was not going to be possible for us. Our lives gradually drifted totally apart, but in a friendly manner and in a spirit of good will.

An ever expanding world was opening up for me. I made new friends who generated more expansive ideas than those put forth in the small isolated community I left. At the same time, I continued to relate well with students and felt that I was their partner in learning; they knew

I was on their side and that I wanted to help them. Working to pull the best from all my students was a creative challenge; inspired by the process of teaching, I wrote a poem about my efforts:

KNEADING
Some people get so much
satisfaction
from slapping and kneading and pounding
bread dough.
As I teach freshman composition
I get so much
satisfaction from
slapping and kneading and pounding.
As I work to inspire students
to think and write,
I see their malleable brains
rising to
delicious heights. .

In my own college experience, I had been exposed to a very few insecure professors who felt they needed to keep students insecure and trembling. I learned from them what I wouldn't do. However, most of my teachers had been respectful and genuinely interested in helping students; these professors now became my role models. As I settled into teaching, the more aware and appreciative I became of those teachers, early and late, who encouraged me, respected me, and instilled in me the confidence that I could learn and achieve worthwhile goals.

My favorite high school teacher, Mr. Blanchard, was certainly one of the teachers who inspired me. I had a growing desire to contact him and thank him for his inspiration and support, but there was a problem. He left Clare High School to return to his home state of New

Hampshire to teach, and I had no idea which city in New Hampshire. Besides, he had moved away over twenty years before I thought about contacting him - he could be anywhere! Still, the idea would not let me go. I began to write a tribute to him for the National Education Association Journal, hoping that the publicity would help locate him.

During the middle of this effort, I had an opportunity to attend an educational conference in Boston with three other Ferris faculty members. We planned to rent a car and extend our time so that we could tour New England. When I shared memories of Mr. Blanchard and talked about my desire to find him, it was suggested that since we would be traveling through New Hampshire, I should look in the telephone books of the cities we would drive through. Although the population of New Hampshire is small, with only a few cities of any size, I couldn't believe that a phone book search would bear fruit. However, I knew l would feel better if I tried to do something concrete toward finding Mr. Blanchard.

We drove into a rest stop as we approached Concord, the third New Hampshire city through which we traveled. I ambled over to a phone booth to check the book, not expecting to find anything. But, under the Bs, I saw two Richard Blanchards listed. One Junior, one Senior. Could it be? I phoned Senior, no answer. I phoned Junior and explained to the woman who answered that I was looking for a teacher, Richard Blanchard, who taught in Clare, Michigan over twenty years ago. "Yes, that's my husband's father," she answered. It seemed incredible that I was actually speaking to the wife of that beautiful baby boy I took care of so many years ago. "Leave the number of your hotel. I'm sure Dad will be home by evening and I'll have him call you," she urged. Later that evening, he did indeed call. "Well, Julie May Ireland, how are you?" his voice boomed. I was very relieved that I didn't need to try to refresh his memory about who I was and overjoyed that he graciously invited our group of four to lunch at his home the next day.

It was wonderful to be able to spend time with Mr. Blanchard, to tell him what his teaching had meant to me, and to share with him that I named my son Richard after him because I had always admired his zest for learning and life. "I am now a successful teacher," I proudly reported, "and I still treasure the copy of the <u>Rubiyat</u> you gave me as a prize for reading Keats' poem, <u>Ode On a Grecian Urn</u>." Smiling, he walked over to a bookcase, reached down to the bottom shelf, pulled out a package and handed it to me. "This is the recording I made of you reading that poem," he said. "I want you to have it now." I couldn't believe he had kept it all those years! Over the lump in my throat, I managed to thank him. After this incredible and satisfying visit, Mr. Blanchard sent me a newspaper clipping announcing that he was Teacher of the Year for the state of New Hampshire. The article pointed out that in all his years of teaching, he never failed to inspire excellence and elicit love from students and those around him. I could testify to the truth of that statement. What an example!

During those first years of teaching, I was diligent in pursuing a degree in psychology and commuted to Central Michigan in Mt. Pleasant to take a class each term. Although outwardly successful and seeming to have it all together, inwardly, I was still a scared little girl looking for a mate to provide emotional security. I knew I needed all the psychological help I could find. I knew that somehow I needed to learn to love and respect myself, and I read books by authors such as Carl Rogers and Eric Fromm in a continuing effort to help myself. I could understand and absorb what they were saying on the head level, but the inner insecurity, the gut wrenching feelings of inferiority never left completely. Also, Richard's death and Robert's institutional life continued to be a weight around my heart.

One weekend, on a retreat with fellow psychology students and our professor, I reached down into levels of dealing with myself not possible in a classroom. I revealed the fantasy that I'd had for years: I walk onto the front porch and begin yelling Richard's name. I keep yelling until he hears me from wherever he has wandered off playing. I yell and yell, hoping he will finally come, and I continue to scream until the men in the white coats take me away. End of scene. Reminding me that other students would be nearby to support me, the professor asked if I wanted to act out the fantasy. "Just yell Richard's name as long as you want to," he suggested. So I began and called Richard's name until my voice gave out, until I was exhausted, finished with it. Then the professor brought out the pillows and instructed me to dialogue with Richard. "I miss you so much! I'm so sorry you're gone! I'm so sorry I wasn't a better mother!" I sobbed. After I finished the dialogue, tears continued to flow. This was the first time I'd felt free to fully express my emotions concerning Richard's death. I wasn't concerned about the reactions of others or fearful they might judge me for being too emotional. I was grateful for the internal cleansing, although I was totally exhausted.

About this time, the women's movement was becoming stronger. I related to it; men, I felt, often treated women unfairly. In my secretarial days I observed capable mature women train the young men who were then promoted over them. I was definitely all for women. I always had close women friends and understood very well the complaints of the leaders of the women's movement. Indeed, Betty Friedan's book <u>The Feminine Mystique</u>, which launched the women's movement, also gave me courage to reach out and take that first secretarial job. Because I wanted to help women find the strength to strive for better lives, I created a women's course, a combination of literature, sociology, and psychology. This turned out to be successful and empowering for everyone, including myself.

Paradoxically, at the same time, I desperately wanted a man in my life and felt less than a woman if I did not have at least an occasional date. There did not seem to be an eligible professor Prince Charming waiting for me, so I decided to try a computer dating service in the Detroit area. I was matched up with "Dr. Bill," a psychiatrist who flew his own private plane. The plane was not exactly a white horse, but when I first saw this very nice looking man climbing out of it at the Big Rapids airport, I was definitely hoping he would turn out to be Prince Charming.

We went out to dinner, and I discovered that he was not only handsome, but also soft-spoken, gentle, brilliant, and best of all, very interested in me. Another whirlwind romance began, and I was off on a new high. I had never been courted by anyone quite like this before. Nothing was too good for me. For my birthday, he emerged from his plane bearing a beautiful set of matched luggage, one piece filled with expensive lingerie and perfumes. Another glamorous aspect of our relationship was the trips we took together in his twin engine plane, - an air show in Pennsylvania, trips to Traverse City to visit Robert, a visit for Colleen to Cedar Point in Ohio, a regional Disneyland.

The next summer, Colleen and I spent time with Bill in Detroit. Getting a feeling for what it might be like married to a doctor, I had fun driving Bill's big Cadillac and noticed there would be a certain amount of spill over respect for the doctor's wife. A few months after we met, Bill proposed, and I accepted. He handed me a book of magnificent house plans and told me he would build a beautiful home of my choosing on a lake near Big Rapids. I felt like my Prince Charming dream was finally coming true.

I was still working on a degree in psychology, and Bill and I talked abstractly about someday working together but never went below the surface in most of our discussions. Because he was often overwhelmed with others' problems in his practice, I felt that I wouldn't burden him with mine. Besides, I was still not able to deal with the pain and shame of my past. I didn't want to disturb Bill's notion that I "had it all together." Because Bill continued to treat me like a princess, I wanted to feel that I might truly be a beautiful and desirable woman after all; I couldn't bring myself to risk his scrutiny of my past. Yet, lurking just underneath the surface was a fear that somehow the dream would not materialize. I panicked when Bill didn't call at exactly the time he said he would, but I did not share these feelings with him.

As time went on, I began to understand more deeply his view of life. He was a Freudian with very definite ideas about the woman being soft and subservient to the man. I came to realize that he too, was very fearful inside himself and wanted a picture book Cinderella wife just as I wanted a picture book Prince Charming husband. He needed someone to love, support, and adore him. However, there was no way to completely disguise the fact that I could not be truly subservient. Yet, we never had a conversation about this. Very much in love with Bill, I didn't want to bring up any possible problems. If Bill saw potential difficulty, he didn't mention it either.

It was a Saturday in September that Bill was due at the Big Rapids airport about noon. When he did not show up or forward a message, I panicked - this time with reason. I asked the airport to check when he left Detroit and was informed that he never left Detroit; his plane was still in the hanger. When I finally heard from him, he confirmed what I already knew. He had changed his mind about our relationship. Period. No explanation or opening to explore why. No process of trying to work it out, no compromise about anything. Just his withdrawal. We both had been quite good at pretending we had it all together. Obviously, neither of us was healthy enough to confront the real issues and deal with them. I was devastated by what I interpreted as another, "you're not good enough for me" message. I thought I was going to die.

Again, everything turned dark. Just when I thought my dreams were about to manifest, they were abruptly dissolved. I didn't feel as bitter and angry as when Duane could not meet my expectations. Instead I felt hopeless, empty, doomed, depressed, not lovable. Somehow I managed to keep going professionally, staying busy with teaching and committee work. Attempting to distract myself from my pain, I ran for the faculty representative body and was elected. My professional and personal selves were becoming more and more separate. Professionally I was productive and active. Personally, I was depressed and lonely.

At the same time, life with Colleen became more challenging. She was not enthusiastic about our move to Big Rapids; it meant changing friends and schools again. Although she made new friends and adjusted quite well in her new school, she was not happy, and especially not happy with me. She was going through what many young girls entering puberty go through, a temporary hostile detachment from Mother! I didn't understand that this was a typical phase, so I felt rejected and emotionally abandoned by her as well as by Bill.

I tried to fix the strained relationship by planning fun things for us to do together. We went on skating and skiing excursions and enjoyed ourselves, at least some of the time. We were clearly going through a rough period. I found it ironic that my students and co-workers believed I was such a neat lady, while my own daughter did not seem to like me very much. I desperately wanted Colleen's love and respect, and I desperately wanted a mate to share my life with; I felt helpless and frustrated in both areas. However, I had incredible drive. I didn't give up easily when I wanted something. I had faith that Colleen and I would eventually be able to mend our relationship and that I would someday connect with the right man for me.

Our neighbor was an older pharmacy student who traveled about thirty miles from Big Rapids to intern in a drugstore. Bud, the store's owner was single, and Bud and Dee dated, fell in love and married. Bud had a newly divorced friend who wanted to meet me, so Bud and Dee arranged a blind date for us. Buck was a former high school coach and biology teacher who ran a successful real estate brokerage. His offbeat sense of humor and zest for life made him fun to be around. We got along well and began to date regularly.

Colleen was included in many of our times together, and we fell into the routine of skiing most winter weekends. Although Jill, Buck's six year old daughter, lived with her mother, she spent many weekends with us, and we enjoyed being a foursome. Colleen and I soon found ourselves with Buck and Jill most weekends that we didn't visit Robert. On Saturdays, Buck was often involved in his office business, so I kept myself busy correcting papers, reading, and spending time with the girls. We usually went out to dinner every Saturday night we were together, and later Buck and I would go dancing. We also enjoyed golf, and played often, sometimes with Buck's parents, who let it be known they would welcome me as part of their family. Buck and I were definitely a couple.

The first Christmas Buck and I were together, he invited Colleen and me to Florida for Christmas break. His parents had a winter home in Punta Gorda, near Fort Myers, so we headquartered there. Buck had a boat there and we stayed out several nights sightseeing, fishing, enjoying Florida. Although Colleen was unhappy most of the time, Buck was very kind to her; she obviously barely put up with him. I realized that she was confused and hurting, but I didn't know how to help her. I hoped that she would outgrow her grumpy attitude.

The next Christmas Buck and I traveled to Florida with Jill. Colleen chose to remain in Michigan to spend Christmas with Duane and Phyllis. Jill and I were becoming very close; just two months previously she had come home from school and found her mother lying dead on the floor. Buck's former wife had been suffering from what she thought was only an ordinary cold; unfortunately, it proved to be a rare form of pneumonia that took her life in only a few hours. My heart went out to Jill; I mothered her as much as I possibly could, and she was very responsive. On the Florida trip we became especially close, and she begged her daddy to marry me so that she could have me for her mother. I was most willing for this to happen because I loved Buck, and I believed he loved me.

There was just one major hitch. He had decided that no matter what, he would not marry again. When we first started dating, he was not direct with me on that issue. He allowed me to believe that, in time, he would be ready for a permanent relationship, but on this trip it was obvious that he was determined there would be no marriage then, or ever. Because I loved him and because I didn't want to be someone's girlfriend for the rest of my life, I hoped he would change his mind. He asked me to move in with him and Jill, but I didn't feel comfortable with that. In spite of the fact that people were beginning to live together without being considered social outcasts, I was concerned about my reputation. I wasn't strong enough to risk possible disapproval, so we seemed to be at an impasse. However, Buck and I continued to spend a great deal of time together, and I kept hoping that he would eventually change his mind about marriage.

CHAPTER SIX
GLIMPSES OF TRUTH

"Nothing can teach you if you
don't unlearn everything first."
-Rumi

Despite being in the midst of a seemingly continuous soap opera, I was about to experience a major turning point. I required a written and an oral book critique of students who took my classes. When student Becky Schaffer began speaking about the idea of reincarnation as described in Ruth Montgomery's book, <u>Here and Hereafter</u>, I was very skeptical. However, I listened attentively because my goal was to teach and model the attributes of an educated person: open-mindedness, and the willingness to listen to divergent points of view. Becky was intelligent and articulate, and what she reported sounded interesting even though I didn't believe it could possibly be true. I was careful to keep a neutral and open expression on my face in spite of making an internal judgment that this was too radical a concept for me to be able to accept.

A few days later, while browsing in the student bookstore, I noticed the Ruth Montgomery book and decided to pick it up to read, "just for kicks some rainy day when there's nothing better to do." A week later, on a rainy day, I had some spare time and decided to look at the book. Because of my avid interest in psychology, I was intrigued to learn that psychologists all over the world use hypnosis to age regress people in order to help them obtain deeper insights into their problems, and that sometimes during this process, people slip back into former life experiences. The book described how the idea of reincarnation can be fit into a Christian framework, how the law of karma operates, and how there is ultimate meaning, love and justice in the universe. I began to get a glimpse of the overall cosmic scheme of things and to feel that perhaps, after all, my life made sense. Perhaps God/Life was not picking on me. Perhaps there was meaning and purpose to it all. Perhaps even if I didn't find THE man for me this lifetime, I would eventually live in love because it is every person's ultimate destiny to do so. Perhaps Richard's death and Robert's circumstances were not just senseless tragedies, but lessons in soul growth for each of us. An inner tugging near my heart signaled the release of the pocket of despair I'd lived with for so long, and I began to sob. Dropping to my knees, I thanked God that just maybe the universe made sense! My serious spiritual journey began in that moment.

I began to understand that our purpose here on earth is to attend Earth School so that we might learn how to extend more love to ourselves and one another. I learned that meditation very often facilitates the process of getting in touch with our true spiritual self, the sacred self at the very core of our being. I was highly motivated to try to meditate on my own but had difficulty. Not understanding how to go about it, I soon become frustrated and shared that frustration with Shannon, a friend and my office mate. Although she hadn't mentioned it before, she now disclosed that she practiced transcendental meditation and recommended it to me. She accompanied me to an introductory lecture, and I was impressed with the scientific studies of improved physiology and psychology as well as the peaceful demeanor of the speaker. I decided to try it.

Because I intended to meditate primarily for the purpose of spiritual growth, I embarked upon a three day fast just prior to the actual instruction time, which deepened the experience for me. After the instruction and first meditation, the world seemed new and different, more peaceful and manageable, and colors seemed purer and brighter. It felt like a motor that had been racing within me suddenly slowed down to normal, only I was not aware of the racing motor until after it stopped. Because I began to notice a difference right away, I was very faithful in daily practice and attended all the follow-up and checking sessions.

Within only a few days, I noticed a degree of understanding and peace between Colleen and me that was not there before. I began to have more tolerance and patience, and our relationship smoothed out considerably. I noticed that my daily highs and lows were not so extreme. When I was happy, it was not the erratic, stressful, hyper-active kind of happiness I so often experienced. When I was sad, the sadness was not as likely to turn into depression. I began to notice that I had more available energy. I continued to read books which explored a spiritual and cosmic view of life, letting go of the more limited concepts put forth by some religious denominations.

I felt wonderful about what was happening to me, so naturally I talked to Buck about it. Not one to miss out on anything, he decided to learn to meditate, too. But from the beginning, he refused to take it as seriously as I did. He made fun of the idea of keeping our personal mantra a secret and began teaching friends or anyone else who wanted to know what he had learned. My life was being changed for the better by meditation, so I was not happy when Buck made light of what was helping me. Yet, we continued to date regularly in spite of this friction.

As summer vacation drew near, Buck asked if Colleen and I would move for the summer to one of the recreational properties he was developing so that I could help in the office at that location. I decided not to be trapped in an office for my summer vacation, and I decided to honor

Colleen's wish not to be isolated from her friends for the summer. Besides, I was continuing to develop a women's studies course, which was a reminder that although I wanted a mate, I also wanted to develop myself as a unique individual. I decided not to be at Buck's heels and at his beck and call. I needed to get on with my own life.

In June I began six weeks of summer classes toward a master's degree in clinical psychology at Central Michigan University. Colleen began her summer by spending time in Clare with her dad and Phyllis. By this time they had four daughters including the daughter Phyllis already had by a former marriage. Colleen enjoyed being around her sisters, and I was happy for her that this was so. However, when she returned home from her visit and asked my permission to live with them and attend school in Clare, I was surprised, incredibly frightened, and panicked at the thought of losing my daughter.

"I just want to be around my sisters and part of a real family," she implored. "We can still visit often - it's only fifty miles away!" I realized that I needed to allow her to try that living arrangement. I was afraid that she would be very angry and resentful if I didn't permit her to at least give it a try. It was difficult for me to speak the words: "You may try it if you're sure that's what you really want, but if you change your mind at any time, you know I always want you with me." The next day at school I opened my heart to the fourteen other people who participated in my group dynamics class. We always sat in a circle because the purpose of the class was to help us acknowledge our feelings and to learn how to be helpful and supportive of each other. The very kind and loving professor- facilitator helped and encouraged us to be authentic. While he permitted confrontation up to a point, he never allowed anyone to get carried away with it. Support and validation for honest feelings was the desired outcome.

I was grateful to the group for the perspective they helped me see. They very much agreed that allowing Colleen to try living with her father was the right decision. They reminded me that living apart for awhile would not necessarily be the end of our mother-daughter relationship. Fortunately, it was quite easy for me to return home from school by a route through Clare. About a week after Colleen's move, I stopped to pick her up for a late lunch. There seemed to be a new and respectful energy between us, and I was grateful. As we talked and shared more openly than we had in months, I saw that our mother-daughter relationship was not only going to remain intact, but actually improve.

With Colleen in Clare, for the first time in twenty-two years, I had only myself to consider. If I wanted to come home and cook, I did. If I wanted to stay out and eat and spend more time with friends, I could. The new freedom was enjoyable. After the six weeks of psychology classes were over, I arranged to go on a month long Transcendental Meditation retreat at Carleton College in Northfield, Minnesota. There, I meditated several times each day, attended lectures, and met many people dedicated to growth in consciousness. The entire experience was peaceful and calming, and I came away with even more faith in the order and justice of the universe.

After returning to Michigan, I dropped plans to obtain a degree in psychology. Although flattered that my professors thought this a mistake, and flattered that they urged me to stay and obtain the degree, I strongly felt this was the right decision. Just a few months of meditation and openness to spiritual growth quieted my inner turmoil and helped me feel safer in the world than all my previous psychological study and work put together. I began to realize that psychology was not the ultimate answer to life's problems, although I knew that I would never stop using and appreciating it. I knew that much growth often comes from it, for me and others, but I knew that in the future I would use it in conjunction with a spiritual view of life. I also knew that I needed more balance and less frenetic activity. Teaching full time along with other responsibilities such as counseling students and attending meetings was enough activity. From the calm and wise center of myself, I knew that pushing to get another degree at this time was not in my highest good.

Continuing to read books about reincarnation, I developed a curiosity about my own possible past lives. A good friend knew Ruth Rebe, a woman in Detroit who had an excellent reputation as a past life reader, so I made an appointment with her. I understood that psychics are not always accurate because information must be filtered through their own consciousness, but I determined to accept only what would feel right for me, and I looked forward to the adventure of this new experience. The ultimate questions were: "Does this information feel right?" "Is it helpful to me now?" One of my concerns was the problem I had finding the right and perfect mate. I was particularly interested in knowing what past connection I had with Duane and why our relationship was so intense and painful. Ruth's reading that day felt very right for me and turned out to be immensely helpful.

Ruth's reading: "You were a general in Hannibal's army. Duane was your wife in that lifetime. You were a male chauvinist who allowed the men under you to rape women. Although you did not participate in the rapes, you were insensitive to women in general as well as to your wife and her needs." This glimpse of a possible past helped me to understand that my lesson in this life might be to experience how women feel when treated shabbily by men. This day I was able to release my remaining anger toward Duane for being such a "poor" husband to me. I began to take more complete responsibility for my own part in the overall drama, to deeply forgive and bless Duane, and to realize we're all souls in the process of learning love.

I also wanted to know how Robert fit into my life. "What horrible thing has one or both of us done to be suffering so much now?" Ruth could not see any specific scenario from the past, but nonetheless offered some comforting thoughts: "Sometimes people agree to come back and live out a situation to learn together. It's not 'bad' karma or punishment, but an opportunity to 'fine tune' the soul, to grow spiritually." These answers from Ruth helped me see that Robert and I were not so much victims as souls who made some choices about lessons in this lifetime.

Although Buck and I were still in relationship, I decided that without commitment on his part, I would eventually choose to end it. I kept putting that off because I kept hoping he would change his mind. Yet, I was becoming stronger within myself as I continued to focus upon spiritual growth. An ongoing issue between Buck and me was my weight. No other man in my life had ever had a problem with the fact that my five feet four inch body weighed 135 pounds. But Buck had an intense dislike of fat - on himself or anyone else. He jogged regularly, even when he was hung over from drinking too much the night before. He constantly harassed me about losing weight. I finally became so agitated by Buck's taunts that I went on a protein only diet and lost twenty pounds. I looked great, but it didn't change anything as far as Buck's willingness to make a commitment. This issue was the indirect catalyst for the breakup of our three year relationship.

Robert had been home for a visit and was to continue on to Clare to spend a few days with his dad. Duane would return him to the hospital in Traverse City. Buck and I drove Robert to Clare, planning to take Colleen and Robert out to dinner and then Buck and I would go dancing afterwards. While we were in Clare, it began to snow, then the snow turned to ice, so Buck and I decided to spend the night at the Doherty Hotel. After dinner we were having drinks at the hotel bar when we ran into a fellow I knew in high school, and he started to rave about how slender and beautiful I looked, and he continued to flirt with me.

My buried anger at Buck's non-commitment and his continual critical remarks about my body came out in the obvious enjoyment of what my friend from high school had to say to me. He was flirting, and I had a marvelous time flirting right back. The more Buck steamed, the more fun I had. By the time we finally went to our room, Buck was furious. I lay down on the bed and began to laugh. I'd had a few drinks and had been holding back my anger for so long, that now I couldn't disguise how funny I thought it was that Buck was jealous and unhappy. It felt great to have Buck see that other men might find me very attractive. I felt I'd proved my point for a change.

However, my laughter was just one blow too many for his male ego. He stomped out and slammed the door. I thought he would probably cool down and be back soon. After a few hours, I began to suspect that he was not coming back. I hadn't brought money with me - only a comb and lipstick. I stayed awake wondering what I'd do if he didn't return before morning. I had no idea whether he had paid the room bill or not. I needed to find out, but it would be embarrassing because this was my home town and a small gossipy one at that.

The next morning when I inquired about the bill, I was informed that Buck did pay it. Then, I phoned a close woman friend who lived in the area, and she came to the rescue. She listened sympathetically to my tale of woe, treated me to breakfast, then drove me home. Two days later Buck showed up with a dozen red roses and an apology. We continued to see each other occasionally after this episode, but it was never the same. We grew apart and our relationship came to an end. I continued to have nostalgic feelings about Buck and Jill and what might have been, and I will always appreciate the good times and fun places we shared. In many ways it was like a three year marriage.

After the relationship with Buck was over, I determined to find other interests. The women's studies class was a source of strength and inspiration. We examined the cultural and psychological factors in women's lives, using literature, readings from psychology and sociology, films and personal experiences. I was the facilitator, learning and growing along with the students. One of the class projects was to write a poem about how the women's movement affected our lives. We then put all the poems in a booklet for everyone to share. I wrote a poem and shared as well:

THE SEARCH

Psychologists say "inner direction"
is important,
But I've found it hard to achieve -
Done too long what is expected
What is applauded.

I've been too concerned about my "image"
and have tried several on for style.
But none of them have been the
me that lies buried under
other's expectations and
my own fears.
Now, some courage and heart
come from the stirring
of my sisters toward personhood.
More courage and heart come from
passing this along to the new
generation.
Oh, dear God, don't let it be
too late for them - or me!

In spite of the fact that I was becoming stronger as a woman and growing spiritually as well, I still could not let go of the idea of a mate and living happily ever after. This fantasy was even more difficult to overcome because I was beginning to feel very lonely now that the relationship with Buck was over. Colleen had been living with her father long enough that the novelty of all that free and flexible time for myself had worn off. Of course, I had work, friends, and other activities, but there was no one to relate closely with on a daily basis. Many gloomy rainy days I came home from school only to sink into depression. There were people I could call, but I didn't want to inflict myself upon them. I began an anti-suicide journal:

> December 1974: I have a terrible enemy - that enemy is inside me. I have met the enemy and it is ME. Somewhere in my unconscious mind there is a black and terrifying monster who wants to see me dead. This monster has managed to keep hidden except for periods of severe stress - until the last few weeks when it is here even when there is no severe stress. Now, this monster - this depression - this hopelessness - this despair - just comes over me with no explanation - no warning. One day I am my normal reasonable fairly productive self and the next day I may be depressed, paranoid, indecisive, useless to myself or anyone else. This has been all the more insidious because so many times during a normal and good period, I have thought, "now I can handle it; now I have a productive course to follow, now it will be ok."
>
> But another bad day comes without reason or warning and I seem to be helpless to do anything about it. There are many friends I could call, but I don't seem to be able to. I think "what's the good of superficial chat-

ter?" or "I can't bother that person." Along with the horrible depression has come the feeling of alienation. I look around and it looks to me like everyone except me has someone to be really close to - not just superficially close. The daily warmth, loving and caring, sharing, fighting - whatever - I miss.

Living alone is bothering me very much. Some people seem to be doing it and thriving, but I can't. Then I think of people who also live alone and hate it - why can't I be close to these people? I think it's going to help me to be able to face this feeling for what it is - an enemy. I have just been cowering, whimpering, and complaining about it until now, but I am going to put up a fight from now on. When this feeling descends, I know I must take action and not just sit and suffer and be paralyzed by it.

I will surely be defeated if I let this prison of the mind enslave me. Sylvia Plath talked about the descending bell jar - when the bell jar or the monster comes after you, the only thing to do is run for your life for that is exactly what is at stake. I've thought about starting a book - my fight with the suicide wish - it might give me a reason for living - maybe it will be helpful to someone. Another thing about the bell jar - it comes down over your head and insulates you - keeps you from communicating with others and then the less you communicate, the worse the depression and hopelessness gets - a terrible vicious circle.

Journal 24 January 1975: our group met last night. (I have reached out and formed a women's support group

- one older woman, one former student I've become close to, and a colleague.) I'm still struggling to find some kind of an answer for the void, the problem.

Some thoughts do occur to me this morning. All my life I've had obstacles to overcome - which has kept me busy. I've been able to say "if I can just do this or obtain that, then maybe I can be happy." There was always a carrot around the corner. I think now I've run out of carrots, or lost faith in them. One carrot has always been "a good loving marriage relationship" - Well, I'm sick and tired of chasing after that carrot. It has just been jerked away too many times. I still go through the motions of searching, but I've lost faith in the whole thing. Somehow I know I've got to find myself and base my life upon something much more endur-ing than that, which is no doubt spiritual truth; then perhaps I could let the rest of life fall into place where it will: "seek first the kingdom of heaven and all the rest will be added."

Obviously, in spite of the fact that I had gained some new spiritual insights, the unhealed areas, the fear of disintegrating into nothingness still haunted me. During the spiritual study of transcendental medita-tion, we were warned that things buried in the psyche would come up for healing as we meditated and became able to handle and heal them. This process was described as "waking up the sleeping elephants so that they might be tamed."

In the midst of the doldrums, in the spring, I decided to go to Hawaii during the two week spring break. Ever since I was a child I'd had the desire to visit Hawaii. I can't remember where or how I first knew about it - perhaps from pictures in books or scenes in movies. I just knew it would be wonderful to be there. I didn't have anyone to go with, so I went with a tour group. A friend and fellow faculty member arranged for me to meet his sister who lives in Hawaii. I also planned to contact Connie, a young woman from Hawaii I met at the TM retreat in Minnesota. On the flight over I met a charming man from Australia, who took me out for dinner and dancing one of the evenings. The faculty member's sister and her husband were very gracious and invited me to their beautiful condo next to the Kahala Hilton. They took me out to dinner and out another evening for a sail on their boat in Honolulu harbor.

I discovered that Connie, my TM friend, was visiting back on the mainland, but her sister Linda and I spent time together instead. With all these activities as well as the activities with the tour group, I had a wonderful first time visit to the islands. The tour group spent a week in Honolulu, three days on Kauai, and three days on Hawaii, the Big Island. I had shown my composition students a dramatic film of Kiluea erupting entitled Heartbeat of a Volcano. It was a thrill for me to actually be there looking down into the smoking crater. My actual experience of Hawaii was a confirmation of the love I felt for it even before I arrived there. It provided joy and healing then and would be very special later on as well.

Back home again and in the routine of things, I began to date occasionally - sometimes a lonely fellow faculty member or someone my friends matched me up with, but nothing came of any of these casual experiences. Lois, a good friend from Central Michigan days, still kept in touch. We were both very open and receptive to finding our right and perfect partner, so we sometimes arranged dates for each other if there was an extra man around. Tom was an older faculty person recently divorced and a friend of someone I was occasionally seeing. I thought perhaps Lois might be interested in Tom.

She came to visit one weekend, and Tom invited Lois, me and my date for dinner. During that dinner I decided that I would like Tom for myself. I'd never met a man like him. He cooked a beautiful dinner and served it in candlelight on beautiful china with the perfect wine. The fire in the fireplace crackled and then glowed as Tom regaled us with his extensive European travel experiences. I was impressed. I was also impressed that he was a sociology professor who was very interested in helping the underdog and that he was involved in politics, active in the Democratic Party. He knew the candidate running for governor of the state. Eventually, he took me to a political meeting at the state capitol where I met Senator Ted Kennedy.

All of these obvious things impressed me, but there was more to it. He definitely was not a handsome man in the usual sense, but he was attractive to me - tall, raw-boned, protruding nose, gray hair. He had a distinctive "stand out in a crowd" look. He sometimes wore a plaid cap, which made him look jaunty and European. Yet it was more than the polish and the looks. There was an intensity about him, a total interest in and passion for life that was the real hook for me.

During dinner that first evening, Tom was polite and interested in all of us. I had no idea about how much he might want to persue a relationship with Lois. I had a feeling that she was not particularly interested in him except as perhaps an extension of her friends and contacts. I knew that somehow I would follow through on my feeling for Tom. Although a part of me feared making a fool of myself, the next Monday I wrote Tom a note and left it in his mailbox at school. It said something about getting caught in a Shakespearian plot, fixing him up with someone else, then deciding I'd like to know him better myself. I stayed home that evening, hoping the phone would ring and it did. From that evening on, we spent time together every day.

Just as Tom and I were getting together, Robert was released from the hospital. He remained in Traverse City as an outpatient for awhile, then moved to Big Rapids into a small apartment of his own. Tom took an interest in Robert, and Robert related well to him. I did not feel so alone in my responsibility. However, it was only a short while before Robert met Lee Ann, a student at Ferris. Her brother was injured in a motorcycle accident and was on medication for seizures, so she wasn't freaked out by Robert's problems. Lee Ann and Robert fell in love and decided to get married just a few months after they met. Lee's school expenses were paid by a trust fund from her grandmother, and Robert collected SSI. Robert did try a few minimum wage jobs, but after he would have a seizure, he would be fired. Unfortunately, his seizures have never been brought under total control. I arranged for him to do janitor work at the mental health clinic in Big Rapids, where the seizures would not be an issue, but Robert's difficulty in relating to people, especially authority figures, became a problem. His hostile attitude soon became too much for the director to handle, so he was fired from that job too. Consequently, Robert fell into the role of house husband while Lee Ann was in school, and that arrangement seemed to work out for them. I was absolutely delighted for Robert, a bit concerned for Lee Ann. It was obvious that they loved each other, but it was also obvious there would be many adjustments as Robert learned to control his emotions.

At the same time that Robert and Lee Ann were getting together, Tom and I were also becoming seriously involved. Tom was not particularly happy with his single life. He had been married to his former wife for thirty years. After the divorce, she moved back to Massachusetts, their original home. Tom's friends were all married. At 62, afraid of being old and lonely, he was ready to try again. Our nineteen year age difference didn't bother me. I felt that finally, after two alcoholics and after Bill and then Buck who couldn't commit, here was finally a truly responsible man. Tom proposed and I accepted. We began working on some cosmetic overhaul of his already nice home and set the wedding date for June. It seemed like a happily ever after story, finally! However, there was much more to this relationship than appeared on the ideal surface. Tom and I were definitely attracted to each other and felt some genuine love as well, but we both had issues and problems underneath all that.

First of all, my attraction for Tom, almost from the very beginning, was accompanied by repulsion. I couldn't understand it; it was like a war going on within myself - push/pull. I found myself disgusted by his frequent nodding off in little cat naps. His driving frightened me; he had "little accidents" like backing into gas pumps. He was truly an absent-minded professor. A part of me saw him as senile and revolting. He was a heavy smoker, and the smoke bothered me. He perspired profusely in his sleep, and I found that disgusting. We had sexual problems. Here again, I was both attracted and repulsed. He was sometimes impotent, which didn't bother me at first because I had total faith in my ability to "turn on" a man. I'd never been with anyone before who had this difficulty, so I was sure that it would be overcome in time.

I convinced Tom it would be a good idea for him to become a meditator since it was so important to me. He agreed, but then fell asleep in every follow-up meeting. He obviously did not share my enthusiasm for meditation. In the midst of all this conflicting emotion, Tom and I were married. I was sure that it would somehow work out. Tom had me on a pedestal - seemed to adore me. I was certain that love would conquer all our problems. We spent several weeks in Virginia and New England on our honeymoon. I talked Tom into attending a week-long conference at the ARE (Association for Research and Enlightenment) in Virginia Beach, the Edgar Cayce headquarters. We had a motel right on the beach. I was thrilled to be there to hear Gina Ciminera and Hugh Lynn Cayce and other spiritual authors whose material I had read. I always enjoyed being around other spiritual seekers. However,

Tom complained about the accommodations and fluctuated between being mildly interested and obviously bored. Somehow we muddled through.

Tom had a better time showing me sights in Virginia where he attended college at Washington and Lee University, and later in Boston where he grew up. Near Charlottesville, Virginia there is a place called Swannanoah where Lao Russell taught spiritual philosophy and exhibited the amazing works of her late husband Walter Russell, known as the man who tapped the secrets of the universe. He was a master scientist, sculptor, painter and author. Tom and I visited this mansion and the grounds there. I was impressed and amazed, but Tom, skeptical and even angry, suggested that this was somehow a hoax. Back at our motel he became angry with me for falling for such "nonsense." My bubble was beginning to burst. I was very hurt that he was attacking me unreasonably. I began to see a facet of his personality that frightened me.

Back in the routine of both of us teaching, things smoothed out temporarily. Tom took charge of the cooking, and I was happy for that. He still liked to give dinner parties. I began to notice that during these parties and during other times we were with people that he spoke for me as though I were a mindless doll. Because he took over and made the plans and decisions for both of us, I didn't feel a part of the planning process, and I began to resent it. I felt like a piece of controlled property. Our sex life was not getting any better, and that aggravated the situation. Tom began to pick fights, and I realized that he was enjoying it when I became upset, especially about petty things.

He frequently told stories about his ex-wife Mary's hysterical nature and how a "good fuck" always calmed her down. I began to realize that Tom was trying to get me to play the same hysterical role that Mary played. In that scenario, Tom was the long suffering good guy; Mary was the screaming sexy shrew that Tom felt good having sex with.

Tom had a classic "Catholic syndrome,"- the bitch, Madonna feeling towards women. Because Tom and I related well much of the time and agreed on many things, and because he truly admired me, I became a Madonna for him, up on the pedestal. However, he couldn't have sex with Madonna/mother. He needed to prod me into acting like a bitch so that he could feel it was proper to have sex with me, but I could not and would not play the bitch role. I didn't discuss these conclusions with Tom because I felt that it would be practically impossible for him to break a pattern of such long duration.

At the same time, I had serious psychological hang ups of my own. I was getting Tom confused with my dad. When I felt repulsed by Tom, the feelings were identical to the feelings of repulsion I had felt toward my father. I was placing Tom in an impossible situation just as he was placing me in one. Although I felt guilty about it, I knew that I wanted out of the marriage. When I told Tom that I felt we should separate, he became extremely upset and threatened suicide. I immediately made an appointment with a psychologist to talk about all this. The psychologist assured me that Tom needed to get help and to be responsible for himself, just as I needed to be responsible for myself. I moved out of the house, but Tom was not finished with me.

He stopped shaving and hung around outside my classroom looking very pathetic. He talked to all of my friends about his undying love and begged them to talk me into coming back. Humiliated and embarrassed, I had no choice but to keep doing my job. When the pathetic tactic didn't work, the crazy phase began. Tom admitted himself into a psychiatric facility in Grand Rapids. One part of me felt like I was the cruelest woman in the world. Yet, I knew that I could not live with Tom again. The pressure was immense because Tom was a friend of the dean of the school where we both taught. I suspected that many people believed I was a bitch for giving Tom such a rough time. So, Tom had managed to turn me into a bitch after all, at least in the eyes of others, if not in actuality.

I became depressed and frustrated and felt totally helpless to control the situation. After one particularly difficult day of deep depression, I decided to end it all. I'd read that a surefire way to commit suicide is to get in a bathtub of water and turn on a radio or other electrical appliance. Crying, I began to run a bathtub of water, but while kneeling beside the tub, I felt as if a hand were grabbing the back of my neck and pulling me up. A message flashed through my mind - "get out of the house - now!" I turned off the water and ran down the street to a friend's house. I sobbed in her arms for several minutes and poured my heart out to her for more than an hour. When our talk was finished, I knew that I would not think about destroying myself again. Perni and I had become friends through our mutual interest in meditation and our dedication to growing spiritually. I was grateful for her love and friendship during this difficult time.

Another blessing during this stressful time was meeting Elaine Davis, the Unity teacher in Big Rapids. Elaine and I were sisters from the beginning conversation, both feeling like we'd always known each other. She invited me to her home for tea and gave me some Unity literature. We continued to see each other often, enjoying each other's company and exploring spiritual ideas.

In the spring I had a visitor from Hawaii. Linda had extended her friendship to me when I was in Hawaii on vacation because I was her sister Connie's friend, and it was a treat to see her. I shared my current frustrations with her and she invited me to come to Hawaii for the summer. "We have plenty of room for you, and you're welcome to come," Linda urged. Images of Hawaii began to dominate my dreams. One morning I awakened knowing that I would go to Hawaii for awhile and that it would be the start of a new life. At first, I planned for the summer, then with the blessing of Linda and of Connie, the sister who owned the home, I decided to extend the time to a year. I asked for and obtained a leave of absence. Then, I sold my car and recreational property I'd invested in. This financed the year away. I was most anxious to put thousands of miles between myself and Tom.

Robert was settled with Lee Ann. Duane and Phyllis lived only a few miles from them and could take care of any emergency. Colleen was graduating from high school and moving to Colorado with her boyfriend. I decided to do what I needed for myself without guilt, which proved to be one of the best decisions I ever made.

CHAPTER SEVEN
A YEAR IN PARADISE

"The spiritual world is like a bird of paradise
flying so close to our eyes that its lovely
feathers brush the pupils, longing to be seen."
- Swedenborg

July 4, 1976 was bicentennial day for the United States of America. People across the country were celebrating our country's freedom and independence, and I was declaring my freedom to direct my own life by embarking upon a year's Hawaiian adventure. I wasn't sure what the year would bring, and some anxiety began to build up on the flight over. "What if Connie doesn't show up to meet me? What will I do then?" I reminded myself that I had credit cards and that I could go to a hotel and re-group, that I could always figure something out. At the peak of my anxiety, I realized that I needed to turn the whole thing over to God. I had memorized the Twenty-Third Psalm and began to repeat it over and over. The anxiety left, and by the time the plane landed, I walked off the plane at peace with myself and full of confidence about the coming year.

Connie was waiting and greeted me with a beautifully scented plumeria lei and drove me to her secluded and peaceful country home. I was beginning to comprehend that my problems were thousands of miles away. I was already feeling much lighter and very grateful for an opportunity to gain perspective. I was ready to heal the pain, frustration, and anxiety that had so recently threatened to overwhelm me. Before this process could begin, however, Connie presented me with another challenge. Connie's living situation had changed; she was now married. Obviously, it was not going to work for me to stay the year with her, but she expected me to stay until something else could be arranged. Some of her TM friends were renting a house together and wanted to find another dedicated meditator to share the house with them. She had already spoken to them about me and offered to introduce us and help in any way she could. For the past several years I'd thought about trying a group living experience but never had the opportunity; I was definitely open to giving it a try, especially because of the focus on meditation.

The group house was in the hills above Punchbowl crater, high up on Alewa Drive. The view encompassed Diamond Head, downtown Honolulu and even beyond that toward Pearl Harbor. Jennie, who would share the downstairs space with me, had her own bedroom and bath but needed to walk through my large room to the stairway. On the other side of the stairway there was another bath and the laundry room. Because of laundry room traffic and Jennie's need to walk through my room, my rent would be only $50 a month, plus my share of the utilities. Impressed by the house and the people who lived there, and grateful for the opportunity, I made arrangements to move in.

Although Jennie had a degree in psychology, she worked as a secretary at the TM center in downtown Honolulu. She had recently divorced after several years of marriage to a Methodist minister, and her three teen-aged children lived with their father. Jennie was warm and fun -loving, and we become good friends and spent many hours together. George, the leader in the house, collected and paid the rent and took overall responsibility for keeping order and peace, but he was a teacher, away for the summer. I would meet him later. Kurt, a law student and Vietnam veteran, was serious and intellectual, yet friendly and fun too. Sally, the daughter of a physician from Chicago, was a TM teacher, and a person I also enjoyed being around. Jana and Lorraine were also TM teachers, but a little more intense and focused on their own lives and problems. Yet, even with all their diversity, the people in the house got along well and were supportive of each other.

We were all responsible for our own meals, had our specific shelves in the refrigerator and cupboard, and had kitchen and house cleaning assignments. Sometimes we cooked and ate a big meal together. It was like living in a family with lots of brothers and sisters. There was relaxed warmth between house members, possibly because we didn't see each other as potential dates. Sometimes we went out together in pairs or in a larger group, but it was always considered a friendly outing, never a date.

During the first month, I rented a car and spent most of my time exploring the island of Oahu. Driving on the north shore, I passed Hawaii Loa College, located back from the road at the foot of towering lush green mountains. They reminded me of accordion pleated dark green velvet. Clouds covered the peaks of the mountains, creating a mystic spell. My heart filled with a longing to teach in that beautiful setting, to be part of that magnificence.

A few weeks later, coming up Alewa Drive after another day of soaking up the beauty on the island, I marveled at the views of the city, the lush flowering trees and shrubs and the lovely tile roofed homes. Every time I drove up that hill, my heart overflowed with gratitude that I had the opportunity to live in this Hawaiian paradise. I was looking forward to meeting George, our house leader, who was scheduled to be back that day. Although I didn't know much about him, I knew that he was divorced from his Japanese wife, that they were still good friends and that they had two children, a boy and a girl, who sometimes spent time with him.

George was at the house when I arrived, and we began to get acquainted and to share our backgrounds with each other. I was surprised to learn that he was an English teacher and that he taught at Hawaii Loa College. I said that I, too, was an English teacher and expressed my admiration for the beauty of Hawaii Loa. "When I drove by, I had a tremendous desire to teach there and to be a part of it, but I know that's a pretty impossible dream," I acknowledged.

"Well, maybe not so impossible," George answered. "I'm the head of the English Department, and it happens that we need a part time teacher right now. Why don't you fill out an application?" he suggested. Everything about Hawaii had been magical so far, but I didn't dare get too excited about this. I made a trip to the college, obtained the application and filled it out. A few days later, to my delight and amazement, I was hired to teach two classes, which would keep me busy three mornings a week and provide some modest income. I purchased a used yellow Pinto wagon in excellent shape with low mileage and air conditioning. I was truly settling in.

I loved Hawaii so very much and rejoiced that it seemed to love me in return. It was a relief to be an ocean away from all those personal pressures. My daughter was the only person on the mainland who knew my telephone number. I did not want to be harassed by Tom or by any problems concerning Robert and Lee Ann that I could do nothing about. Jennie and I discussed my feelings of frustration about Tom, and she shared the concept of <u>release</u> with me, something I'd never heard of before except in a physical sense. Tom had obtained my address from Robert and was sending me mail and packages, which I didn't want and complained loudly about. "If you want him to leave you alone, and if you want to be at peace about him," Jennie said, "you must forgive him and let go of your strong feelings of resentment. All that energy and frustration keeps you bound to each other." Her comments served to remind me of the truth that I knew, but had not been practicing, and I began to seriously work on forgiving and releasing Tom. I must admit that this task was probably accomplished only because we were an ocean apart, and he was not breathing down my neck or causing immediate embarrassment.

Jennie and I tried the Unity Church near Diamond Head, and we both loved it. The side walls opened to allow the flower scented gentle breezes to gently caress the congregants. The message of love and hope was empowering, and I began attending many of the classes and activities, as well as every Sunday service. On one very special Sunday a few weeks later, I joined the church. My good friends from the house were there and presented me with a beautiful maile leaf lei to go with the plumeria lei from the church. It was a very moving and special occasion for me.

With only part time teaching, I had plenty of time to relax and to read, and I particularly enjoyed re-reading James Michner's Hawaii. It was a thrill to occasionally glance up from the book and look at Diamond Head while reading descriptive passages about how the eruption of that volcano formed the island of Oahu. I was inspired to explore as much of Hawaii as I possibly could during the time I would be there. I went through a ship anchored in the harbor the missionaries had sailed in, which had been restored and turned into a museum. I drove through the pineapple and sugar cane fields and recalled Michner's account of how these enterprises changed the simple life of the Hawaiians. I spent several afternoons in the Bishop museum and made several excursions to Chinatown, always basking in the Aloha spirit of the people and the perfect climate.

Relaxing on the beach at Waikiki several afternoons each week was a regular routine. I remember one lazy afternoon in particular. I'd moved my straw mat up under a palm tree out of the sun. My swim had been fun and relaxing, and I pulled out Gail Sheehy's book, Passages, from my beach bag and began reading where I had left off. Several of Sheehy's descriptions of life phases had helped me understand my own often erratic life. The idea that if we miss a phase or passage at one time in life, we usually try to go back and pick it up later, helped me understand my intense desire for a stable home and a loving man. I'd never experienced a stable home for long, and a stable loving partner had thus far eluded me. As I continued reading, I was surprised and delighted to find my current situation described: "Somewhere between 35 and 45 if we let ourselves, most of us will have a full-out authenticity crisis." She went on to discuss how sometimes even people with successful careers go off to places like the South Seas to find meaning and purpose. She was talking about me! It felt wonderful to read a description of my current situation and to be reminded that what I was going through was not so different from what many others experience. Validation was satisfying, and I laughingly reminded myself, "Maybe I'm not a nut case after all!"

This magical place was certainly providing me with an incredible opportunity to find meaning and purpose for my life. I had a built in family and support system, as well as all the time I needed and wanted for myself. Any potential crisis-producing people and situations were several thousand miles away. Layers of stress and anxiety continued to melt away. However, I was still carrying around all those unresolved yearnings and dreams of the right man and happily ever after. I was not actively seeking anyone, and in fact was very satisfied with a lull in my love life - but the lull in that area turned out to be short-lived.

I loved meeting new people at church, both men and women. One Sunday after church, I chatted with Joe, a very sweet and friendly older man. When he asked me out to lunch, the thought flashed across my brain, "prepare for more." That intuitive message proved to be correct. Although Joe was obviously much older, I was impressed with his dynamic energy and his youthful and enthusiastic attitude toward life. He often brought his young friend Bob to church with him. Their routine was to have a light lunch after the service and then go to the park and throw a softball. At their invitation, I joined them on these excursions. I discovered that Joe had a wife who was not interested in church and not interested in his spiritual pursuits. Although Joe and I were obviously attracted to each other, we agreed that we were and would remain "just good friends."

However, as we continued to get to know each other better, the more difficult it was to be "just friends." We spent hours telling each other about the events in our lives before we met, and I was fascinated by his life journey. He knew and actually worked with Napoleon Hill, author of <u>Think and Grow Rich</u>. He knew the spiritual teacher and author, Joel Goldsmith, and attended his meetings at the YWCA in Honolulu. He had been on an active and sincere spiritual quest for many years. We always had a multitude of things to discuss. His gentleness and warmth, his sparkle and enthusiasm endeared him to me. But there was more. A powerful physical chemistry existed between us, and in spite of the thirty year age difference, we became lovers as well as friends. He began to think about leaving his unhappy marriage so that we could be together, and I wanted that very much. I couldn't think of anything more wonderful than to be married to Joe and to live permanently in Hawaii.

In October, I received a plaintive telephone call from Colleen. She was very unhappy with her boyfriend and uncertain about what she wanted to do with her life. "Come to Hawaii," I urged. "Perhaps we can figure out together what you might do." A few days later, I met her at the Honolulu airport. There was no problem about living arrangements; my downstairs room was big enough for both of us. We obtained another twin bed, a bureau, and a portable screen, which created two rooms from one. The only further financial obligation was for us to pay one more share of the utility bills. It was great to have Colleen with me again. Right away, she decided to take the TM course and began meditating with me, fitting in beautifully with the people and the routine of the house. When Joe and Colleen met, they liked each other from the start; Hawaii was continuing to work its magic.

Colleen tried to find work, but that was impossible. As soon as a prospective employer learned that she had recently arrived from the mainland, that was the end of any interest in hiring her. We decided to just enjoy Hawaii and the time together and not worry about employment for her. We enjoyed the beach, the movies, and Unity church activities. It had been over three years since we had lived together, and we both had changed. We now realized that we could relate to each other as friends as well as love each other as mother and daughter. Our time together was a healing that we both deeply appreciated.

One evening during these months of feeling more and more peace and contentment, I was blessed with a transcendent experience: It was twilight and I was alone in the house, relaxing on the lanai, enjoying the panoramic view of the city and the distant ocean. The first lights of the city and the lights of the harbor ships began to twinkle like tiny jewels. I'd been reading Eric Butterworth's book In The Flow of Life, and the uplifting message was expanding my heart and mind. As I looked out over the beauty before me, I felt a part of me leave my body and float out over the city. My heart overflowed with love and gratitude for the beauty before me and for the perfectly orchestrated symphony of life.

After I found myself back on the lanai, I remembered the Robert Frost poem, Desert Places, and how in the past I had lived in desert places in my mind and heart because I didn't know any better. I didn't have the opportunity to experience the Paradise Places I was now experiencing in Hawaii. Frost's poem describes his feelings while looking into an empty snow covered field with a few weeds and stubble showing through. He feels sudden loneliness and emptiness that he expects will just get worse because underneath it all there is nothingness. He was scared of the desert place inside himself, just as I was so often scared of the "void" within myself.

However, this time in Hawaii had opened up for me an answer to Robert Frost in the form of my own poem,

THE PARADISE PLACE:

Life flowing, and I knowing, fast oh fast
In the Hawaii space I live in, going past.
The city twinkles its lights, and the sea
Massages and nurtures the shores.
The seekers here have it; it is ours.
All nature bursts forth in joy with us.
I am inspired to praise and thank God
For endless blessings.
And wonderful as these blessings are,
The endless waves of joy will climb higher and higher,
A brilliant catalyst of life, creating itself in
Endless expression - having everything to express.
The despair we sometimes feel when we imagine
Empty Spaces is the God-created emotion that propels
Our unfolding self to seek and to be one with the
Magnificent loving and true Reality - God the Creator
Who dwells in our hearts

At that moment, tuned into this truth and feeling so much peace and harmony, I couldn't imagine feeling anything else again. But because I was not yet enlightened, I soon experienced other more challenging emotions as well. During the closing months of our time in Hawaii, I began to feel some concern and anxiety about Joe and our relationship. A breakthrough came one night when we were out dancing. Joe was an accomplished dancer who had taken ballroom dancing lessons; he had been dancing regularly for years. I loved to dance but had never taken lessons or danced regularly. Joe and I danced adequately together and enjoyed it, but I was not that smooth. On that particular evening, we ran into some people he knew, including a very attractive woman who had once danced professionally. When Joe asked her to dance, I didn't think too much about it until I realized they were staying on the floor and continuing through several numbers. I was sitting alone at our table.

Beginning to feel quite angry and jealous, I went into the ladies room to regain some composure. While attempting to hold back the tears, an affirmation I learned at Unity came to mind: "What is mine by Divine Right is mine and cannot be taken from me. If it's not mine by Divine Right, I don't want it anyway." I began to say these words over and over to myself, and I felt calm and at peace; I knew that I could relax. "I can trust the Universe to unfold the situation perfectly," I thought. "I can know that if Joe is mine by Divine Right, nothing or no one can keep us apart. If not, nothing will hold us together." I truly loved Joe and wanted his highest good as well as my own. I went back to the table where Joe was waiting for me, and we enjoyed the rest of the evening dancing together. He did not even realize that I had been upset.

After that experience, I still felt some tension because I was not certain what would happen in the future. Yet, my faith was building - I knew I could trust a loving God - I knew there was ultimate justice. I only wanted what was best for everyone. Joe decided to talk to his attorney about a divorce and what it would mean to him financially. The attorney convinced him that it would be foolish for him to think about divorce at his age, that he would lose too much, and that it would be too difficult for him in every way. Joe and I discussed this and decided that his attorney was probably right. Joe suggested that I stay in Hawaii. He would pay for an apartment, so we could still be together as much as possible. However, I didn't feel comfortable with that kind of arrangement. Colleen's future was also an important consideration. She had decided that she would like to go on to school. Any job I might get in Hawaii would not pay enough for me to help Colleen through school, and I would not allow Joe to do it. Besides, she had decided that she would prefer to go back to the mainland. It made sense for us to return to Michigan. I would resume teaching at Ferris, and Colleen could live with me and attend school there.

Colleen left Hawaii a month before I did in order to have time to visit her father and her other family. Joe and I spent a great deal of time together that last month, and he even flew with me to San Diego where we enjoyed a few days together before I returned to Michigan. We continued to talk on the phone, to write, and to send tapes to each other. After about two months, Joe told me that he was being torn apart. "Perhaps it will be easier for both of us if we stop communicating and try to get on with our lives,'"he suggested. I understood that and agreed with him. So, with mutual feelings of love and understanding, we stopped communicating. Of course, we didn't forget each other, nor were we finished with one another yet.

CHAPTER EIGHT
PUSHING THE LIMITS

"The infinite and eternal are just outside
the limits of your cage. The soul is infinite,
free to expand everywhere."
Michael Singer

At the beginning of summer 1977, I returned to Michigan feeling rested, relaxed, and renewed from the year away. Before returning to Big Rapids, I decided to stop over in Detroit to buy a car and to visit my "sister" Ruth, my birth mother. My feelings about Ruth were mixed, but I was interested in bringing about a closer relationship with her. Although she was my biological mother, we had always related to each other as sisters. I felt compassion for her because she had a very difficult childhood as well as tough times as an adult. Her first husband left her and their two boys for a younger woman. She then married a man who beat her. Finally, she met and married Ben, and this marriage lasted for many years. However, he gradually lost his sight from Retinitis Pigmentosa, an inherited eye disease, so the family was forced to deal with financial pressures as well as the frustration of Ben's blindness.

After I began to delve into psychology and to look at life in more spiritual terms, I was ready to look more closely at my early life. I wanted to talk with Ruth about the hardships of our childhoods. I wanted her to say, "I love you, and I wish our lives could have been different." But she was uncomfortable when I brought up the past and attempted to delve into some of my feelings about it. She became defensive and asserted, "I had it rough too!" This was indeed true, and I could listen and sympathize with her, but she could not do the same for me. The child in me felt put down, discounted and resentful. I knew Ruth loved me, and I loved her, but there was a barrier between us.

Ruth had three sons, two from her first marriage, and one from the current one. I loved all three brothers, but they were never told the truth about me and always related to me as Aunt Julie, although Ruth did reveal my true identity to her husband. My favorite brother was the youngest, Ben. He too majored in English, had a Master's degree, and loved teaching. He was very loving and outgoing, sensitive and fun to be around, and so far, not married and living at home. When I returned from Hawaii, Ben drove me around Detroit and helped me pick out a new car, a bright red sporty Ford Mustang. I invited him to come with me to a Sunday service at the Unity church in Warren, and we were both moved by the inspirational message of love. I began to realize that I very much wanted him to know that I was actually his sister. I came very close to telling him as we drove home from church, but felt I should not do this without Ruth's permission. Later in the day, I discussed it with her. "I'm not ready for Ben to know," she declared, "I just can't handle it right now. It would be upsetting for my husband because he doesn't want any of the boys to know about it." With those words, some part of my heart closed. I felt like a "dirty secret" that must not be exposed. After that, I decided to protect myself by keeping some emotional distance from Ruth and Ben.

Later that summer, I traveled to Unity Village, near Kansas City, Missouri, for the purpose of taking some classes. These classes were not a part of ministerial training, but a separate program for people who wanted to deepen their knowledge of Unity philosophy. People who took these courses often became licensed Unity teachers, minister's assistants who could teach classes and counsel in a unity church. My dear friend Elaine had gifted me with the funds to stay an extra session, so I was there a whole month. I was impressed by the beautiful grounds and the rose gardens and fountains and Mediterranean architecture, but most of all I was impressed by the atmosphere of joy and friendliness, the dedication to a higher and better way of living. It was an enchanting place and a unique time where my spiritual life deepened and new horizons and possibilities opened to me.

The time at Unity Village deepened my growing desire to become a Unity minister. I observed a glow emanating from Unity people that seemed to reflect inner peace and joy. Whatever they had, I wanted to have it too. I decided to become involved in the Grand Rapids Unity Church, even though it meant a 120 mile round trip from Big Rapids each Sunday

On the fourteen hour drive back to Michigan from Missouri, I listened to a tape by Ruth Carter Stapleton, president Jimmy Carter's sister. She talked about the pain that many people carry because they have never felt loved or wanted, and then she described how she works with people to facilitate their inner healing. The miles flew by as I listened to stories about the people she has helped. I continued to drive and listen as Ruth led the listener into a guided visualization. "See the room where you will shortly be born - see it filled with light. Mary and Jesus are there to welcome you because you are so very precious and special. When you are born, they rejoice. They hold you, and their loving light enfolds you and welcomes you." I pulled over to the side of the road and began to sob uncontrollably. This was release, not anguish. I had finally been welcomed to the world!

I was blessed with another positive and life-changing experience when I stopped in Midland, Michigan to visit Barbara, a classmate from Central Michigan days. Barbara was the publicity director for the united Way based in Saginaw, and she had some tickets to a seminar by Elizabeth Kubler Ross, the psychiatrist who had done extensive research on the stages of death and dying. I knew about Dr. Ross' work and was happy for the chance to hear her speak. The meeting was held in a huge auditorium, and most of the people in attendance were doctors, nurses, and health care professionals. I was prepared to be impressed. However, when this middle-aged little lady with thinning hair, wearing what looked like a house dress walked out on the stage in front of over two thousand people, I began to feel sorry for her and wondered how she would be able to cope with such a large audience. I didn't wonder for long. Elizabeth began by sharing her experience working with dying children. It was necessary to listen very closely because she had a thick accent. She also told us about her life growing up in Switzerland and about her struggle to survive being born a two pound triplet.

She was forced to develop incredible strength in a home that didn't value the contributions of girls. After World War II, when she was only eighteen, she traveled around Europe on her own, helping to clean up the rubble. Eventually, overcoming many obstacles, working and finding financing on her own, she became a doctor. She later came to the United Stated States and married an American doctor. During her residency as a psychiatrist, she worked in some of the worst mental institutions in New York. She found what would be her life's work when she began to investigate the thoughts and emotions of dying people. She heard many accounts of their near death experiences and many accounts of their glimpses of an afterlife. A mutual love and respect grew between Elizabeth and her patients.

Elizabeth reminded us of the necessity to understand that the dying process is an important passage in a person's life. Dying people need to be listened to and interacted with, not shunned because of our own fears. Dying people shed the superficial and get down to what is truly important. We can learn from them. Elizabeth's accounts of the wisdom of dying children deeply moved me. But Elizabeth did not stop there. She told several stories that underscored the idea that in truth there is no death. We shed our body, our Earth Suit, but our essence continues on. I was flabbergasted when she began to discuss the idea of guardian spirits and angels and her own experiences with entities from the other side. After all, we were sitting in a room filled with over two thousand scientists! One statement in particular hit home for me. "Don't worry about your loved ones that have gone on," Elizabeth said. "They often stay near you as guides - their loving presence is with you right now." The moment after I heard Elizabeth's words, I heard Richard say, "See Mom, I told you I'm OK. I love you; I'm with you." I accepted the truth of this and savored this sacred moment, saying nothing to Barbara.

After the meeting, we stood around in the lobby talking to some of Barbara's friends. Everyone had been held captive by Elizabeth's dynamic presence. In spite of her startling ideas, I heard no doubts or put downs. After a few minutes had passed, Barbara said, "Julie, I have a feeling that Richard was with you today." I could only nod in agreement. The day felt so special that I wanted something tangible to symbolize it, so we went shopping, and a purchased a carnelian and silver hand crafted ring which served to remind me of Richard's presence.

Back in Big Rapids, I rented a two bedroom apartment near campus and purchased some new furniture, so Colleen and I were ready to begin the new school year. It was good to be back. Colleen and I continued to get along with each other wonderfully well. Appreciating the opportunity for higher education, she was dedicated in her studies. Robert and Lee Ann were still living in Big Rapids, and Lee Ann continued to take classes at Ferris, so our family was together again.

Although Colleen was uncomfortable driving in Honolulu, she was ready to practice her driving skills in the less challenging area of Big Rapids, so I encouraged her to drive more. One evening, she asked if she could take a drive to Clare. "I won't stay long, and I'll be back later tonight," she promised. I hesitated, the nerves tightening in my stomach; for some reason it did not feel right for her to go. But what I thought was my common sense told me, "Stop being an overprotective mother - let her go." A few minutes after she went out the door, the nerves in my stomach went wild yet again. In a panic, I grabbed the Daily Word, Unity's little magazine that has an uplifting thought for each day of the month. I read this and began to meditate, seeing Colleen protected and returning home safely.

Just a few minutes later, the phone rang: "Mother, I've just wrecked the car. They are taking us to the hospital for x-rays, but I'm alright." The downstairs neighbor drove me to the hospital, and I saw that Colleen was indeed going to be fine. I listened as she explained how she crashed into the back of a truck that was stalled in the middle of the road without its tail lights illumined. The Mustang was beyond repair, totally wrecked, but Colleen walked away. I realized that I needed to listen more carefully to my intuition, and I thanked God for answered prayers.

My interest in the Women's Studies class was still strong, and I was able to resume teaching it. I was delighted that both Colleen and Lee Ann could take the class from me. The few men who enrolled learned that the women's movement could be beneficial to them too, and the women students learned to be stronger women. I certainly benefitted from the class myself, perhaps even more than the students. The more I taught the material, the stronger I became. I reached an understanding that most women dream of "Prince Charming and Happily Ever After." It goes deeper than any one woman's personal history. This myth is deep in the culture, and we all need to examine it and understand it; otherwise we continue to be controlled by an unreal mirage. However, at the time, although I understood this only in my head, it was a first liberating step for me. It would be a few more years before I could integrate it emotionally and be truly free of the idea that a woman is incomplete without a man at her side.

Back on campus and into the routine of teaching, it was inevitable that I would encounter my professor ex-husband. I had mellowed, forgiven and released, so I was at peace about him and had let down my defensive barriers. He wanted to be friends, I agreed to that, and we went out to dinner occasionally. He seemed recovered from any mental problems, but I felt I need to set definite limits. "We can be good friends, but nothing more and definitely no attempts at sex," I insisted. He accepted those boundaries.

At the same time, I felt free to see anyone I wanted and to go out with others occasionally. Tom began to invite me to go on little trips out of town, separate beds of course. There was not much of interest outside the college in Big Rapids, so it was not difficult to allow myself to accept those invitations. Besides, I genuinely enjoyed his company when he was not crazy and demanding. I found myself spending more time with him, and in spite of myself, getting caught up in his plans and expectations.

On the other hand, I hadn't lost sight of my spiritual goals. I was still traveling to Grand Rapids to attend the Unity church. My friend Elaine and I decided to start a Unity study group in Big Rapids. We met on Tuesday evenings, listened to a tape, and then Elaine and I led a discussion. Once a month, David Drew, the minister from Grand Rapids, came up for a potluck supper and led a class. In addition I decided to develop some meditation and personal growth workshops. Everything I did was geared toward spiritual growth and preparation for the Unity ministry.

In the spring, Tom asked me to accompany him on a trip to England. I agreed to go because he understood that our relationship was to remain platonic. We traveled for three beautiful weeks in England, Scotland,

and Wales. I was amazed at the beauty of the English countryside, fascinated by London, and grateful for the opportunity to visit Findhorn in northern Scotland. Findhorn, a spiritual community founded by Peter and Eileen Caddy became famous for its bountiful crops produced on barren sandy soil. The community believed their oversized vegetables to be a result of the cooperation of nature spirits. We enjoyed one afternoon there and one afternoon at the While Eagle Temple in southern England. However, Tom was more interested in historical sites than the esoteric ones, and since he was paying for the trip and acting as guide, we basically followed his agenda.

In spite of some disagreements and tensions, and in spite of having to drive on the left side of the road, which often resulted in my screaming with fear, it was a beautiful trip. The highlight was seeing Ingrid Bergman in a stage play in London. We had marvelous front row seats in the side balcony, right over the stage. I leaned over the edge and never took my eyes off Ingrid. She was my childhood idol, and still the actress I most admired. I was thrilled to be so close to her, and had the outrageous thought, "she's so close, I could spit on her head.!"

About a month after we returned from England, I gave in to the necessity of a hemorrhoid operation at the famous Ferguson-Droste hospital in Grand Rapids. The hospital specializes in rectal operations, and many people from all over the world go there when they need this type of surgery. I was aware of the body-mind connection and realized that someone in my life was sometimes a "pain in the ass." I was also aware of the importance of maintaining a positive attitude. Before and after the surgery, I listened to soothing tapes of harp and flute music and visualized light and healing energy flowing through my body. I was thankful for minimum pain and a rapid recuperation.

The next school year brought much the same routine as the previous one. Colleen and I continued to enjoy living together, and she continued to do well in her studies. I remained involved with Unity while maintaining a friendly relationship with Tom. During this time, I was becoming increasingly dedicated to the pursuit of psychological and spiritual growth. As good as teaching was for me, there was something missing, although I did bring important issues to the students to think about and write about, such as aging and discrimination, and any other issues I felt would deepen their capacity to care more about others.

Whenever the opportunity arose, I attended spiritual retreats with friends. On one of those retreats, I met George and Florence Champagne. George and Florence had traveled to the Philippines where George experienced a dramatic healing, and they had brought back amazing films of the Filipino healers at work. The Champagnes and I became good friends, and I invited them to talk to my students and show their film. The students were free to scoff or disagree, but they were challenged to open their minds and consider unusual possibilities, and they seemed to appreciate the opportunity to do this. My relationship with the students continued to be very good because I truly cared about them and extended support and encouragement. Although I was not an official minister, I ministered to the students in ways that perhaps a minister with the title could not.

Although Colleen and I were having a wonderful time living together, I knew her time with me would have a limit; she would soon graduate and get on with her own life. I began to even more seriously explore the possibility of a new career in the Unity ministry. I had a desire to be more intimately involved with people, and I wanted to live in an atmosphere where pushing my personal limits would be natural and expected. In the academic world, I felt some of my colleagues looking askance at my psychological and spiritual explorations. I believed the Unity ministry would offer a loving support system composed of people whose aspirations matched mine.

I talked to my minister about the idea, and he agreed to advise and help me with what was sometimes a complicated procedure. I sent for the lengthy and detailed application forms, the required reading list and other materials to study. Part of me felt like an imposter because I knew full well that I was not totally whole and healed. However, naively I believed that once I became a Unity minister, I would find myself miraculously whole and healed by the process.

As I became more focused on my new goal, I felt the need to at least partially disengage myself from Tom and his expectations. After careful thought and prayer, I told him, "I want to remain friends and to see you for dinner and other activities, but I can't go on any more trips with you." I knew this was going to be disappointing to him because he had a San Franciso trip planned for us, but I was not prepared for his reaction. In spite of the fact that I was empathetic and willing to listen to him, his emotions got out of control, and he fell apart, exhibiting the same crazy and threatening behavior as when we divorced.

The next afternoon as I was working in my office at school, Tom, obviously agitated, walked in and announced, "I'm going to phone Unity Village, and I'm going to talk to Charles Fillmore, the president of Unity School, and tell him what a terrible person you really are! He'll never allow you to get into ministerial school!" Those words cut through me like a dagger. Some part of me believed Tom's assessment of me. When he finally marched off, he left crying and shaking, terrified that he would carry out this threat.

I rushed over to Elaine's house, and this dear friend spoke words of truth I needed to remember. "Neither Tom or anyone else can keep you from becoming a Unity minister if that's what Spirit knows is for your highest good and for the good of all." I also phoned my minister and poured out my distress to him about Tom's threat. I received a comforting message of truth from him as well. "People at the village would not take seriously anything ex-husbands would have to say," he assured me. "You know I will vouch for you, but I don't think it will come to that." The panic receded as I focused upon a more positive outcome.

However, within a few days I developed a sharp pain that ran between my shoulder blades, through my chest, and down my arm. I feared a heart attack, but a trip to the emergency room and an E. K. G. ruled that out. The pain was intense at night when I lay down; aspirin couldn't even touch it. A glass of wine only made the pain worse. I sat up many nights, getting very little sleep and spending extended time in meditation.

I made an elaborate image book because it was impossible to sleep with the pain, and the book project helped keep my mind on something positive. My image book was a scrapbook of pictures and words that depicted what I wanted to do, to have and to be. I put together sections affirming Unity Minister, Successful, Wealthy, Perfect Relationship, Health of Body. This kept me focused on what I wanted and helped me release physical pain and emotional anxiety. I understood the body-mind connection with this pain, which came right after Tom's threat, a threat that was like a knife cutting through my heart. Eventually, the problem was diagnosed as a haital hernia(later an ulcer), which I learned to manage and keep under control.

When Colleen graduated from the executive secretarial program, she decided to move to Houston, Texas. Houston was at the height of its boom. Bill and DeVere, Colleen's aunt and uncle, lived in Houston, and invited her to come and stay with them until she could find a job and get settled. Duane and Phyllis came to the apartment with a U-Haul trailer and drove Colleen and her furniture and personal belongings to Texas. I had long since let go of any animosity toward Duane and in fact felt very loving toward him. I still sometimes regretted that things hadn't worked out between us. During those times of wanting to go back and re-live the past, I wondered if we might have stayed together if I'd obtained a college degree and pursued my own interests. Of course, I couldn't let these emotions show. Our lives had taken different turns. He and Phyllis continued to be heavy drinkers. When I saw him and I got that "old feeling," I slipped into nostalgia and wished things had turned out differently, but at the same time, I realized that if I were faced with the everyday reality of living with a drinker again, it would not be possible for me to handle it.

Colleen's Uncle Bill worked for ARAMCO Oil Company, jointly owned by Saudi Arabian and American companies. Bill and DeVere had spent several years in Saudi Arabia with the company, but Bill was based in Houston. Bill took Colleen into the personnel office and helped her obtain an application. Within a few months she was making more money with her two year degree than I was with a Master's and eleven years of college teaching experience! Nonetheless, I was very happy for her and a very proud Mom besides.

After sending in the application for ministerial school, I waited anxiously for the results of the first screening, which would determine whether or not I would be called for an interview. Between four and six hundred people applied each year, eighty were invited for interviews and further testing; forty were eventually accepted for school. I was still affirming that "what is mine by Divine Right cannot be taken from me." I kept praying Tom would not phone Unity Village and that if he did, he would not be taken seriously. I also prayed he would find another woman to care about so that he could release me without further trauma for either of us. Finally, I received a letter inviting me to the village for interviews. So far, so good!

The experience at the Village was positive. It was great to meet the other candidates. Although we were somewhat in competition - only half of us would be accepted - we were still very supportive of each other.

Each of us had a thirty minute interview with a panel of experienced ministers, who would then prepare a written statement about what they believed our aptitude for ministry might be. In two weeks we would be notified by mail about the outcome. The three ministers who interviewed me were very mellow. There were two soft spoken women ministers, one of them, after she discovered I was from Big Rapids, said that she knew Elaine Davis. I knew it was going to be a plus for me that we facilitated a study group together. The man, Charles Roth, was older. It felt strange, yet very satisfying, to realize that Rev. Roth looked like and sounded like Joe, my Hawaii love. I was comfortable talking with him because I felt almost like I already knew him. I hoped our rapport was a good omen predicting my eventual acceptance into the program.

After the interviews I returned home to await the outcome. In an attempt to come to a friendly and normal relationship with Tom, I had allowed him, when he asked, to drive me to the airport in Grand Rapids and to pick me up upon my return. While at the Village, I continued to pour forth heartfelt prayers that Tom would release me and find another woman. Nevertheless, when I walked off the plane and saw him with a woman, I was surprised. He introduced me to Erika, a sociologist he'd just met; they were obviously attracted to each other and planned to spend time together. I felt incredibly thankful to be released, - and happy for Tom.

About two weeks later, THE letter from Unity was waiting for me when I returned home after school. I was afraid to open it, dreading the terrible disappointment if the answer was "no." Yet, I knew God would be with me and show me the way, no matter what. I sat for awhile and meditated with the unopened letter in my lap. Finally, with trembling fingers, I opened the letter and read it. The answer was "yes!"

Overjoyed, I began to make preparations for the new direction in my life. I gave notice at school and was given a year's leave of absence "just in case" ministry didn't work out for me. Although I did not ask for this leave, I appreciated the school's willingness to offer it. They ended up extending the one year to two years - again without my asking. By selling my furniture and shipping books and pictures ahead to a friend in Kansas City, I was able to pare down to what would fit in the car. There was a room waiting for me in the women's hotel on the Village grounds. In order to earn a little extra income I signed up to teach an evening English Composition class at Longwood, a nearby community college. Everything seemed to be falling into place beautifully.

CHAPTER NINE
CHANGES CHALLENGES AND SURPRISES

"Life may not be the party we hoped for,
but while we're here, we might as well dance."
- Tom Stoppard

Busily and happily preparing to make positive changes in my life yet again, I was aware that change - wanted change - was exciting and energizing. Who could know what wonders the future might bring? Along with those thoughts of how everything needed to be organized for making a smooth transition into the next adventure, persistent thoughts of Joe kept flashing through my mind. Charles Roth, the mellow and kind interviewing minister, had reminded me so much of Joe. I realized that I would very much like him to know I had been accepted for ministerial school. Joe and I had discussed at length my desire to become a Unity minister, so I knew he would be very proud of me and happy that my dream was now coming true. "Just one phone call to tell Joe my good news won't disrupt his life," I convinced myself.

But as I reached for the phone, a strong intuitive message stopped me: "If you do this, you'll get more than you bargain for!" I hung up the phone and decided to think carefully before I made a contact. However, as my departure for Missouri neared, a persistent facet of myself that wanted to talk to Joe became increasingly restless. "Come on, one little phone call won't hurt -you only want him to know what you're doing." Finally, the urge to talk to Joe won out over the original intuition advising caution.

My hands were a little shaky as I dialed Joe's number in Hawaii. I expected his wife to answer the phone, so I was relieved when he answered right away. "Julie," he exclaimed. "I was just thinking about calling you! My divorce was just final." It was wonderful to hear his voice and to hear his surprising news. "I'm going to be in Chicago in a few days to visit relatives," he continued, "Will you meet me there? I'd love to see you." Although a part of me felt anxious about this disruption in the smooth flow of my moving preparations, I was thrilled at the prospect of seeing this dear man again, and I agreed to meet him a few days later.

Three years had gone by since Joe and I had seen each other, but the years fell away the moment we saw one another. From our first hug, it became obvious there was still a strong attraction between us. However, there was a difference in me. Although my feeling for Joe was indeed strong, I had an even stronger determination to become a Unity minister. Joe was certainly very supportive of that goal, but early in our whirlwind of dinners, dancing, and meeting friends and relatives, he began to talk about how he could support me in the ministry if we were married. "I'd enjoy just staying in the background and being your cheerleader," he professed. "Besides, he added, "you wouldn't have to worry about money - I'd support you in every way; you could just think about getting through school."

One part of me embraced this idea, but another part was afraid that if Joe and I married, I might not be able to follow through with the necessary hard work demanded in the ministerial training. I was thrown into deep inner turmoil, pulled two ways at once. I wanted to be with Joe, but in the three years we'd been apart, I had made a new life for myself which included a strong commitment to a new goal. I'd worked long and hard to get this near it, and I couldn't just abandon it, no matter how much I loved Joe.

Then, in the midst of the turmoil, I remembered the rule Unity had in place for people entering school. No newlyweds, no newly divorced people. A year must elapse between any marriage or divorce and a person's entry into school. I feared that if Joe and I married immediately, I would have to wait a year before starting school; I feared that something might happen that I would not begin at all. When I explained the year rule to Joe his response was, "Julie, you know I'm not getting any younger, and we can't know how much time we'll have together as it is. We've been apart three years already. Please, let's not wait."

Although my heart melted, I still couldn't surrender my goal. "You know I love you too, Joe, and I want us to be together, but I must follow through with ministerial school." A strong energy inside me would not allow me to give up the pursuit. However, even as I spoke these words, a compromise occurred to me. "Perhaps we can go together and talk to the director of Unity school and explain our situation to him," I suggested. "If he will make an exception in our case, we'll get married now. If he won't make an exception, we can still spend as much time together as possible and then get married later." Joe expressed his willingness to go along with this plan of action.

Joe had been a very successful salesman and a public relations person for many years, so he knew how to state a case, and I could be quite persuasive myself. The director of the ministerial school was an open-minded, kind, and flexible human being. Joe and I explained to him that if we were married, my time in school would be so much easier, that Joe would support me all the way, that our marriage would be made in Heaven. We truly believed this. The director was convinced, and he agreed to make an exception in our case.

There was a part of me that still felt uneasy because my careful and precise plans were being so abruptly changed, but what we had worked our seemed reasonable. I made a determined effort to lay my misgivings aside, reminding myself, "Having Joe as well as the opportunity to begin ministerial school makes you a very fortunate woman, Julie." Gradually I relaxed and experienced the joy and excitement of a bride-to-be.

It was then early June. School would begin near the end of July. Joe accompanied me to Texas to tell Colleen our news. Colleen and Joe had always liked each other, so Colleen was delighted to see him, and happy for both of us that we were finally getting together. We stayed in Texas a few days then drove back to Kansas City and rented a lovely apartment near the school. We'd worry about buying furniture later. We had decided to fly to Hawaii to be married and to have a brief honeymoon there before school started.

We arranged a dream wedding in the courtyard of the Unity Church near Diamond Head, the church where Joe and I met. Elva Elsner, a licensed Unity teacher and a good friend with whom I'd shared ideas of becoming a minister performed the wedding ceremony. Jeanne, another friend I'd met at the church three years earlier, was my matron of honor. George from our TM group house attended, but other friends from the house were no longer in Hawaii. Jennie was living in San Francisco, and I planned a short visit with her on the way back to Kansas City.

After the afternoon garden wedding in the Unity courtyard, we floated ecstatically through a sunset reception at the beautiful and historic Royal Hawaiian Hotel. Later, we drove to the Turtle Bay resort on the north shore for our honeymoon. Enjoying the spectacular ocean views, breathing in the fragrance of tropical flowers, dining and dancing in luxury hotels, I felt like the star of a 50's Technicolor musical romance.

Joe and I had two relaxed weeks together in Hawaii before it was time for me to fly back to the mainland to ready our apartment and prepare for school. Joe remained in Hawaii for three more weeks after I left, putting his affairs in order so that he could leave for an extended period.

A part of me found it difficult to leave Hawaii and my new husband, but another part was eager to dive into the new adventure in Kansas City. However, the San Francisco stopover was a treat for me because it was wonderful to see Jennie again and to share my "happily ever after" ending with her. She had been a confidant and support system for me during the time Joe and I were dealing with the complications of falling in love, so it was wonderful to see her again. She was working in one of the offices at Berkeley and had an apartment there, so she knew San Francisco well and was a great tour guide. We shopped and ate in Chinatown and visited Ghirardelli Square and Fisherman's Wharf. I purchased a unique copper and bronze mirror from Egypt at Gumps, a famous import store full of treasures from around the world. The two day visit seemed more like two hours.

When I finally flew into Kansas City, I encountered record breaking heat and humidity. It had been over 100 degrees for days and didn't cool off much at night either. It was draining to be out at all, even though stores and autos were air conditioned. Having sold most of my own things, I didn't have much to contribute to a new household. It was great fun to buy several rooms of furniture and accessories all at once - to try out my skill as an interior decorator and to create a beautiful and comfortable living environment for Joe and me as we began our new life together.

When school started, I reconnected with some of the people I met during interviews and began to make new friends as well. Our class was comprised of forty people whose ages ranged from the early twenties to the sixties and who came from many different professions and life experiences. Yet, because we were all gathered for the purpose of becoming Unity ministers, for this time and space we shared many of the same concerns and ideals. James Dillet Freeman, head of Silent Unity and a well known metaphysical poet, welcomed us to Unity School. However, in his welcoming speech, he warned, "If there is **Anything** else you can do, you'd better leave now and go do it! Ministry is only for those who absolutely cannot do anything else." Seemed like a very strong statement then. I thought he was being a cranky old man, but the day eventually came when I agreed with him

Our class schedule was from 8:00 am until noon, Monday through Friday. Studying, along with extracurricular activities such as hospital and prison work, and work with area churches was scheduled for afternoons, evenings, and weekends. In the weeks before Joe arrived, I enjoyed spending as much time as possible with my new friends, three other single women with whom I related very well. There was a marvelous compatibility between all of us - Vivian, Sonja, Helice, and me. It seemed important to us in this adjustment period to discuss what was going on in our classes, to discuss the teachers' expectations of us, and to share our fears about being able to meet those expectations. We decided to form a Master Mind prayer group. Jack Boland, the minister in Warren, Michigan who had been instrumental in promoting these groups was visiting the Village and was happy to join us for our first meeting, which was a real thrill for us. We met every week, shared our concerns, and allowed the Spirit of Truth to speak through us in a supportive way for each other. We also found that laughing, relaxing, and just being silly together was a part of the bonding process and a great stress reducer as well.

It seemed no time at all until Joe arrived. He brought a huge bouquet of red anthuruims from Hawaii. The next morning I wore one of these big red waxy flowers in my hair and proudly took him to class. Spouses were allowed to sit in. Joe especially enjoyed the speech class because of his own avid interest in public speaking; however, our teacher did not appreciate his expert comments, which made it a bit awkward for me.

Joe was a person who loved people and who had been the center of attention in his group of friends and associates in Hawaii for the previous twenty-five years. I soon realized that it was going to be a difficult adjustment for him to be in Kansas City where he knew no one but me. His difficulty in playing the role of tag along husband to a ministerial student was obvious. Moreover, he did not have business to attend to in Kansas City, nor did he become interested in other activities. He came to class with me, or waited for me to return home so that we could do something together. We were regulars at the swimming pool, and we occasionally invited other couples for dinner, but I was having a difficult time adjusting to his needs I had been single for ten years, except for the six months I was married to professor Tom, and I was used to coming and going as I pleased. Feeling a bit confined, I felt the need to carve out space for myself by lunching with my classmates instead of going directly home after class and by arranging to study some afternoons on campus.

Everyone was feeling the effects of the merciless 100 degree heat wave, with no relief in sight. One afternoon as Joe was walking around campus looking for me, he became overheated and disoriented. A classmate helped him find me, but later asked me, "What are you doing with this man, Julie?" The implication was that Joe was senile and that our relationship was not appropriate because of our age difference. My own ego boundaries were not very solid. Too vulnerable to other people's opinions, I had a need to be liked, accepted, and approved of, especially by my classmates whom I considered to be very wise and special people. A part of me began to have doubts about our age difference; a part of me began to feel embarrassed by Joe. He felt my emotional distance and consequently made a few additional demands on me I did not have time to cook a complete dinner every night, so we often ate out, but when we didn't eat out, we settled for sandwiches and pick up foods. Joe decided that he was tired of sandwiches and demanded that I do more cooking. I made an effort, but resented it and complained to my friends about his demands.

I felt guilty that I was not paying more attention to Joe, but on the other hand, the time consuming study was essential. Besides all that, there was another factor involved. I was feeling strongly the need to fully establish my own identity and direction. Joe had promised, "I'll take a back seat; I'll be your cheerleader." I knew he meant to keep his promise, but in the real situation, it was not so easy for him. I loved Joe, but I was finding the pressures of school and a new marriage a tremendous challenge. I believed I could meet this challenge if I could hang onto a certain degree of autonomy, if I could be free to express myself without having to be fearful of Joe's reactions.

Our underlying conflict came to a head one evening when a classmate and his wife decided to have a party. They lived just two buildings from us in the apartment complex, so Joe and I walked the short distance. Once there, we enjoyed the company of the other students, their wives and some faculty members. Toward the end of that Friday evening, the host invited those of us who might be interested to stay and listen to some special metaphysical tapes, and I decided to do that. However, Joe wanted to go home, and he wanted me to go home with him. "Just go on if you're tired," I suggested, "I'll be along a little later." I saw that he was not happy about my decision, but I felt it was a reasonable one. I felt compelled to prove to myself and to Joe that I was a free person, that the marriage was not a cage separating me from my friends.

Joe left, not at all happy, and about an hour and a half later, I walked back to our apartment and found him furiously pacing the floor, obviously very angry. Although Joe was not normally a person who cussed, some prime swear words came out of his mouth. He ended with the ultimatum, "A wife leaves a party when her husband does! No wife of mine is going to treat me with such disrespect!" It was the beginning of the end. A few days later we came to a mutual conclusion that the marriage was not working under the present circumstances. I realized that if I would leave school, if we would go back to Hawaii together, if I could let ministry go and be more of an old fashioned wife, we could probably stay married. However, I was not willing to leave school or give up the goal of ministry, even though I truly cared for Joe. I had not always liked him during the past few weeks, but I knew stress had brought out the worst in both of us. Joe decided to return to Hawaii and file for divorce. The marriage lasted a little over two months. I remembered the intuitive voice I heard before I called Joe the first time from Big Rapids: "If you do this, you're going to get more than you bargain for." Yes, indeed

Teachers and fellow students rallied around. After the apartment lease was up, friends helped with the move into the women's hotel on the village grounds. Again I asked for and received a part time teaching position at the community college. I settled into being a single and serious student. I tuned out men except as casual friends. Helice, Sonja, Vivian and I gathered every Friday evening for our prayer session and then went out to dinner or a movie. We had wonderful times together, and we truly appreciated the mutual support.

About this time my friends and I saw and appreciated the film <u>Ordinary People</u>. I received a very personal message from it concerning my son Robert because of the theme of this movie. The mother in the story was fixated on the idea of perfection, for herself and for those in her family. Her eldest son had died while living out the role of perfect son and achiever. She could not get out of her self-pity and her fixation on that eldest son. Consequently, she failed to appreciate, love, and nurture her remaining son or her husband. She reflected for me some of my own lack of acceptance for my son, Robert. I had never completely stopped grieving over the fact that Robert was handicapped;

I had difficulty accepting the fact that Robert could not lead a completely "normal" life, that I could never refer to my son as the achiever whose accomplishments might enhance my own self-esteem. Before I saw this film, my attitude was so mixed in with the pain I felt for Robert that I couldn't recognize my own self-pity or my view of him as "somehow inferior."

Mary Tyler Moore, who played the mother in the film, laid it out for me on the big screen, and I experienced a shock of recognition. I knew that I wanted to change, that I wanted to accept Robert totally and unconditionally just as he was. The next day, after a cleansing crying session with my support group, I phoned Robert. Although I often told him, "I love you," this day I said the words from a truer and deeper space within myself, meaning that I loved the entirety of him, just as he was, problems and all.

In a continuing effort to confront more of the buried issues in my life, I started counseling with Martha Guidici, one of our teachers. I wanted to confront the shame around my childhood sexual abuse. Although I wasn't comfortable sharing it all, it was a breakthrough step. Martha responded with a statement that gave me a whole new viewpoint. "Julie," she assured me, "your experience is not that unusual. As you heal, you will be able to minister to many others with the same problem." I began to take the focus off my shame and to understand that one day I could use my experiences to help others in their recovery.

During the second year of school, I was thrilled to be hired as a student minister in Columbia, Missouri, 125 miles east of Kansas City. This allowed me to give up teaching at the community college and to focus totally on ministry. The Unity group met early on Sunday evenings, so I left Unity Village about three every Sunday afternoon and returned about eleven at night. The two and a half hour afternoon drive to Columbia provided time to go over my talk and the class I would teach, to listen to inspirational tapes, and to sort over the experiences of the week.

One Sunday afternoon as I was driving merrily along, focused on my note cards and practicing my talk aloud, I felt like I was on automatic pilot. I'd set the cruise control at seventy and believed I was driving safely enough on the flat and straight freeway. Suddenly, I became aware of being tail-gated by a police car! I had no idea how long I'd been so closely followed while driving five miles per hour over the speed limit and not really keeping my eyes on the road. At the same moment I noticed him, the policeman turned on his siren and lights and pulled me over.

Realizing there was no point in pretending innocence, I accepted the ticket and promised to slow down and pay more attention to my driving in the future. Although I was not happy about the $25 fine, I felt the universe had given me a valid warning. I certainly did need to be a more careful and responsible driver; I wasn't ready to leave planet Earth quite yet. The people at church had fun teasing me about this experience. An elderly lady obviously enjoyed warning me every Sunday evening for the remainder of my year in Columbia, "Watch out for the cops on the way home."

The two and a half hour drive back to Unity Village was unwinding time. I always taped my talks, then listened to them in the car and critiqued myself. I wanted to do a good job of ministering to those people at Unity of Columbia who were so very appreciative of whatever I presented to them. Stevens College and the University of Missouri are located in Columbia, and many of the church people were connected with one of the schools; being a former college teacher, I felt comfortable and at home with them. The year with the Unity group in Columbia was one of growth and loving connection. However, the group was small and not yet quite ready for a full time minister, so as graduation neared, it was necessary for me to send out resumes to other places.

One of the culminating activities for us was the writing of our credo, our current belief system and world view. We were given specific categories to discuss, such as man's situation on planet earth, man's problems, and perhaps most important of all, man's possibilities and relationship to God. The following are some brief excerpts from my credo:

> When man is born, he chooses the time, place, and circumstances in order to learn certain lessons. The SITUATION is that he does not remember why he is here. This forgetting is part of the challenge he has set up for himself; he believes he has no control over his circumstances. He sees his inner world of thoughts and feelings separate from the world which acts upon him, and against which he must defend himself. His primary motive is survival, or escape from suffering, or pursuit of pleasure...

One of the most powerful books I ever read is FOR THOSE I LOVED by Martin Gray. Gray was a fourteen year old Polish Jew in Warsaw when the Nazis took over. His story is one of intelligence, energy, courage and love under horrible circumstances. Gray fought for his family and himself, for life when all those around him had given up.

He did not tell his story in religious terms, but the book still had a powerful unspoken spiritual message. His passion was to save lives and to live to create more life; he looked beyond unspeakable horror to love and to hope. Yet, when we discuss man's situation, we are including men like Gray who fight for life and men like Hitler who are determined to end life.

Dr. Elizabeth Kubler-Ross says we all have a Saint Theresa and a Hitler inside us. She believes it is important for us to acknowledge that. I have discovered that it takes a tremendous amount of courage to be able to acknowledge the Hitler in me, and I could only begin to do it after I began to experience the divinity in me. I now realize that I must look at my own dark side and heal and transform it so that the truth of myself, the Christ Self may express. Martin Gray's story helped me to put my own life in perspective. It reminded me that he, and many others, had the strength and the courage to go through much more than I could ever imagine. They demonstrated a triumph of the human spirit. I knew that I, too, needed to keep on pushing forward, to not give in to despair.

Man's POSSIBILITY is limitless because he is inherently good; he is an expression of God whether he knows it or not. There comes a time for every soul, in some lifetime, when he is ready to grow spiritually, when he asks for, prays for, and sincerely desires a better way. As Unity writer Emile Cady says, "it is in God's fullness of the time." Then man is ready to learn about his true nature, to choose the high road, the spiritual path. He begins the awakening process. I believe Martin Gray's experiences brought him to that point, and I feel that my experiences in this lifetime have led me to seek and find a spiritual path. For that I am immensely grateful.

The ultimate possibility, and the inevitability, for man is to understand and to express his divine nature. I believe he can live in harmony, peace, and joy, that he can enter into the kingdom of heaven and that he can begin to do so here and now. CONCLUSION: I dedicate myself to doing everything I can to help myself and others express our Divine nature. I will counsel, teach, and give talks, but perhaps most importantly, I will strive to make my own life one that "works" by surrendering to Spirit and letting the Christ light shine through me. Unity's founder, Charles Fillmore said, "More truth and love is caught than taught;" thus, I will try to be as contagious as possible.

Two months before our ordination, a very dynamic and friendly couple came to Unity Village. Steve was applying for ministerial school, but he was also board president at Unity of North Idaho in Coeur d' Alene. He wanted to convince some of the graduating ministers to send resumes to his church. His slide presentation was effective. It depicted the beauty of the area and the unique meeting place of the church, a small chapel which is an historical monument built by General Sherman of Civil War fame. The surrounding mountains and lakes also looked spectacular. I was very interested.

I had never been to Idaho, so I decided to send in my resume and, if invited for an interview, to see some new territory. Shortly after they received my resume, the church invited me to Idaho for an interview. I noticed that the Unity church was across the street from North Idaho College, which was pleasing to me because I always appreciated a college atmosphere. The people in the church seemed loving and dynamic, and the area was indeed beautiful, so I decided that if asked, I would accept a position as their new minister. About a week after I returned to Unity Village, Steve called and offered me the position, and I accepted it. I'd be going to Idaho in July; in fact my fast Sunday there would be on the 4th. I remembered the momentous bi-centennial July 4th that I spent traveling to Hawaii. I couldn't help but feel very positive about the upcoming Idaho adventure. It was then only April. I was fortunate to have the pressure of placement over so early.

My excitement around the June ordination was incredible. I had graduated and completed things before, but this event was the symbol of my highest aspirations. I had dreamed about this and made sacrifices to attain it. I was overjoyed that I was finally becoming a Unity minister. The ceremony itself felt very sacred - God Himself/Herself seemed to be saying to me, "Go, Julie! Well done!" I expected my life to only get better and better. On this euphoric high, I temporarily forgot that continued learning experiences are an inevitable part of Earth School.

CHAPTER TEN
WESTWARD HO!

"There are no mistakes and there is nothing lacking.
We're always going to get what we need,
not what we think we need."
Byron Katie

The time span between ordination and starting the new ministry in Idaho was only three weeks. Because the church had been without a minister for several months, the board was anxious to have a minister on the job. I'd been on such a high for the past few months I didn't realize that it might have been wise to arrange for some rest and a space between school and the responsibility of a full time ministry. Full of energy and enthusiasm for my new adventure, I neglected to accurately access the limits of my physical endurance or the relentless demands of a full time and growing ministry.

While in school, I had sent for an Astro-Cartography chart, a map of the earth divided into different zones. The premise was that, based on an individual's birth chart, different geographical areas can provide unique lessons and energy. Michigan, for me, was a Saturn zone. Saturn, a planet of challenges and difficulties, has been called the taskmaster planet. My experiences in Michigan seemed to verify this. An area extending through Albuquerque, New Mexico and curving up through Spokane, Washington is a Venus zone for me - a place where I should experience pleasure, appreciation, love and support. Just the opposite of my Michigan experience! The astrologer included a personal note with my chart: "Moving from Michigan into a Venus zone would be like moving from a dungeon into Disneyland." Coeur d'Alene, Idaho is only thirty miles east of Spokane, Washington, right in the center of my Venus zone. I was about to discover what effect the energy in this zone would have upon me.

However, I needed to make a trip to Michigan before heading west to Idaho. Mom was recuperating from a heart attack that had taken place just two weeks earlier. Because it was so close to graduation, and because the prognosis was that she would recover, I didn't leave school at the time, so I was anxious to spend several days with her. She was at home and doing well under the circumstances, but the doctor ordered her to slow down. Somehow I expected Mom to be the same forever, to do all the cooking, cleaning, and playing cards late at night just as she always had. "But now she's over seventy," I reminded myself, "and she's had a heart attack." I wanted her to understand just how much I loved her, and she seemed to comprehend the depth of my appreciation for her. She had exuded a love and sweetness that attracted loving friends all her life. During her convalescence, the many visitors besides my brothers and myself included her stepchildren, Ruth and Beulah.

My brother Ben accompanied his mom and dad in order to see his grandmother and also to see me before I left for Idaho. I had decided during the long drive back to Michigan that I would talk to Ben and say to him, "I'm your sister, not your aunt." I was willing to risk Ruth and Ben's anger about this. However, I was scared and nervous about my brother's reaction. Would he tell me he didn't want to have a relationship with me? I felt that it might be too much of a shock, too much of a problem for him. There was a city park only a block from Mom's house, and I asked Ben to go for a walk with me. On our walk, I began to lead up slowly to what I was about to share. "Ben, I have something I need to talk to you about. I don't know if you're going to understand, but it's important for me to tell you this." All the while I was trying to prepare myself for rejection if it happened.

Ben's manner was easy and relaxed as usual, but he seemed interested in what I was going to say. Finally, I just blurted it out: "Ben, I'm not really your aunt - I'm your sister! Many years ago your Mom had me when she was just a young girl. She couldn't keep me then, so I lived with Grandma Florence until I was adopted by Grandpa and Grandma Ireland." I checked Ben's face for his possible shock, but saw only his usual kind and interested expression. "I haven't told you before because your mom and dad weren't comfortable about your knowing. But, Ben, you are so special to me. I've wanted you to know our true relationship for quite awhile, only I didn't want to offend Ruth and Ben, or upset you either." "Julie, I'm delighted that you're my sister," he beamed, giving me a big hug. Relieved, I began to cry. We agreed to keep our conversation confidential until the "time was right" to share it with Ruth and Ben. It felt good that Ben had accepted me, and it felt good to have summoned the courage to tell him the truth, to be vulnerable. A comforting message flashed across my mind. "You are a beautiful human being, worthy of consideration; you are not a dirty secret."

The long drive to Idaho, which I began a few days later, provided many hours for me to gain perspective and review my life. At the same time, I was treated to majestic views of America and often found myself singing America the Beautiful. However, as I drove across the Mackinaw Bridge into upper Michigan, I was reminded of the time when Duane and I drove across it in a hearse with Richard's body I the back. Twenty years had gone by since his death, and there had been a certain amount of healing on my part. However, I could at times still feel incredible pain and guilt. In spite of this, I had faith that Richard was always near me, helping me as a guide from the other side, encouraging me to stay focused on a spiritual path, and I was grateful for the sense of loving connection. The drive along the sandy shoreline of Lake Michigan on highway 2 in Upper Michigan was beautiful and relaxing, but I continued to feel a residue of sadness about Richard, a sadness that the drive across the bridge had triggered. But then I suddenly felt Richard's presence encouraging me to appreciate the dance of the bright blue waves and the billowing white caps. It was almost as if he were whispering in my ear: "Allow the pain of the past to fade so that you can open your heart to the joys of the future." I determined to take his advice.

Coeur d'Alene, Idaho, July 1982. Tired but happy to be here, I zealously pushed myself to exhaustion as I settled into a new apartment and dove into the work at the church. At first, I had no idea why I felt so dizzy and tired, why I often needed to force my body to get out of bed in the morning, so I concluded that I was probably adjusting to the change of altitude. It would be awhile before I figured out what I really needed, - a restful vacation. Steve, the board president at the church, had been accepted into ministerial school, and he and his wife would leave town soon, but they were available at first to welcome me. They took time from their moving preparations to take me on an afternoon excursion on their boat, and we toured Lake Coeur d'Alene and went water skiing. I was happy for Steve that he had been accepted into school, that he was going to do what was best for him However, after he left, I'd be dealing with the present vice-president, a woman who, I discovered later, was not happy that I was selected as the new minister.

During the -first weeks, things at the church seemed to go well, and attendance and offerings increased. Unfortunately, just as I was beginning to feel more acclimated, Mother had another heart attack. Her doctor urged me to return to Michigan immediately if I wanted to see her again. Extremely distraught and feeling I had no choice, I asked the church board for time off to make the trip. However, I knew all this was going to put me in a financial crunch, and complicate my relationship with the board.

In the midst of this dilemma, two women church members who had invited me to their home for dinner, and who had been friendly and supportive in every way, stopped by to see me. We heard about your situation and want to give you money for your trip; this is a gift, not a loan," they announced. I was deeply moved and grateful for the kindness and generosity of my new friends, Ione and Masil. They told me about their prayer work with people who come to their healing center for help They offered to pray with me, and we saw God's healing light surrounding my mother.

Back in Michigan, Mom and I shared once more how much we loved and appreciated each other. I told her repeatedly, "I can never repay you for the love and stability you gave me, Mom; you are so precious to me." Her answer was always, "and you are so precious to me Julie." We talked about death. "I'm not afraid" Mom assured me. "When it's my time, I'm ready to go." However, she was open to prayer and to seeing the healing love and light of God moving in and through her, and miraculously, she began to recover. It was not her time to die after all. As soon as she was discharged from the hospital, I returned to my work in Idaho.

I was challenged to continue to push myself. It was time for the western region minister's conference, which had been scheduled by the previous minister to take place in Coeur d'Alene. Much time and energy was required to complete the arrangements and to act as host minister to the hundred and fifty people attending. The five day conference went smoothly, and I was thankful I was able to disguise the exhaustion that was threatening to incapacitate me. On the surface, all was well. Attendance and offerings at church were still increasing, and many members expressed their appreciation, complimenting me about what a good job I was doing for the church.

In spite of loving support from the congregation, I began to receive complaints from two women on the board, the president and the secretary. They were unhappy because I didn't spend as many hours in the office as they felt necessary. I soon discovered they were complaining about me to others as well. I called them in to talk and to pray in an attempt to stop any negativity before it damaged the ministry. Our session seemed to go well, but I soon discovered they were continuing to say nasty things about me to members of the congregation and continuing to complain about my absence from the office.

I felt it most important to get the job done well, not sit in the office for hours whether there was anything to do or not. I believed community involvement outside the office to be important for the church and for the minister. However, that was not the belief of these two women on the board. I was invited to present my views on prayer and meditation to a group in the community. "This is a good opportunity to help the community know about Unity," I enthusiastically reported to the board president. "It's all set for next week!" I couldn't believe it when I was told, "You need to ask our permission to do these things." Of course, I went ahead with what I felt was right. These incidents were only the beginning of the petty and nasty incidents that followed.

In the midst of all this stress and hassle, Ione and Masil invited me on a three day trip to the Oregon coast. We planned to leave Sunday after church, and I would be back before the Wednesday evening class. The board president told me sternly, "You can't go." Fighting words for me, I answered, "You can't tell me that," and the battle was on. She called a special board meeting for after church on Sunday. To present my case, I prepared a chart of what had been accomplished since I arrived at the church in Coeur d'Alene, and laid out a plan of action for the coming months. After a lengthy and stressful meeting, the board finally decided it was permissible for me to take an extra day off once a month. Ione, Masil, and I left late that afternoon for the Oregon coast.

Nonetheless, I continued to feel so much ill will directed toward me from the president and the secretary of the board that I realized I couldn't possibly continue to work with them. All the energy spent in bickering was energy taken away from the good of the church. I asked the ladies to resign and they refused. Without my knowledge, they talked to the Unity minister in Spokane about how unreasonable I was. They were not about to gracefully retreat, so the battle intensified. A part of me wanted to find a way out of this mess.

I decided to call Joe in Hawaii and to find out what was happening in his life. Joe was happy to hear from me and happy that I finished school, but he also had some news to share with me. He was happily remarried to a woman he met at a dancing club. She was happy to stay home and to make him the only focus of her life. "I'm so happy for you Joe!" I exclaimed, and meant it, managing to disguise the fact that I was not so happy for myself right at that moment.

As the stress of the church battle became increasingly disruptive and miserable for everyone, many of my staunch supporters at the church suggested that we start another Unity group, walk away from the nastiness and start over. Ione and Masil were willing to provide major support for this effort with the understanding that the group would soon become self-supporting and affiliated with Unity.

I knew that several other Unity churches had divided into two groups, and I naively believed that it would be no big problem for us. I couldn't quite get over the shock of discovering that Unity people could be nasty, especially Unity leaders elected to boards. I thought I was in a very unique situation and that I would be doing Unity and the peaceful people at the church a big favor by helping them form a separate group away from the people who wanted to fight. I wouldn't be able to see for quite some time that I was actually caught up in a power struggle and a no-win situation. Although I'd benefitted greatly from the study of <u>A Course</u> <u>in Miracles</u>, and I knew that "defenselessness is strength and defenselessness is where my safety lies," I was still "caught in the drama.

However, before I could move ahead with any plans for a new group, before I could allow Ione and Masil to commit to its major support, I felt an obligation to tell them about my past, especially the four marriages. In spite of considerable healing, I was still ashamed of my past and feared I was not worthy of their confidence. "I need to talk to you before we go ahead with any plans; there are things you should know about me that you may have trouble accepting," I declared. Over breakfast and extra coffee, I began to outline my past, including the marriages. "Is that all?" was the response. "We thought you might have done something really awful! All these things you've shared don't matter to us. You are a beautiful lady and we love and support you." I was truly touched by this. The part of me that harshly judged myself was surprised, and I wondered, "Can it be that what I've found so necessary to hide from others is not so terrible after all?" It was great to have such loving and supportive people around me. We decided to move ahead with our plans to begin another group.

I was in for many shocks and lessons in reality. The placement director of Unity ordered me back to the village and suggested to the Coeur d'Alene church board that they fire me. All this triggered my righteous indignation. I stayed put, and we started the new group anyway. Steve phoned from the village and begged me to leave Coeur d' Alene; he sounded like he was in pain, too. I felt like a deer mesmerized in the headlights of an oncoming car. I was so tired. I didn't have energy enough to travel across the country and to start all over. However, the most important reason for staying was a sense of loyalty to Ione and

Masil and the others who were supporting me. I felt that it was too late to back out of my commitment to them.

Even so, my insides were going crazy. I began to feel horrified that I'd managed to get myself into such a controversial situation. I began to doubt myself and my own sanity. One day, I would decide to give it up and return to the Village; the next day I would decide to see it through. In spite of my anguish and turmoil, over one hundred people showed up on the first Sunday, eager to be part of a new group, and everything went along quite smoothly. At the same time, because I was in trouble with the Unity administration, I was grieving mightily. Some part of me feared I'd done something very wrong; another part believed I had taken the best action under the circumstances. I certainly didn't want to do anything to hurt Unity - I loved Unity. As a result, my heart and commitment were not totally with this new group.

On the other hand, I loved Ione and Masil and the people in our group, so I felt the torture of being pulled apart. After a few months, some key people sensed my lack of commitment and decided to pull away; the group gradually became smaller. Ione and Masil had been the main support, and when it became obvious that the group would not become self-supporting, we decided to let it go. At the time we formed the new group, I had moved out to the Holo Center, a few miles north of Coeur d' Alene. This was Ione and Masil's private home, which also housed their counseling and healing ministry. They invited me to remain at the Center and to assist them in their work, and I decided to do that.

Ione, Masil, and I had come together by divine appointment. The similar circumstances of our lives were quite extraordinary, we felt. I was adopted when I was nine; Ione adopted her son Alan, whose background is very similar to mine, when he was nine. Masil adopted all three of her children, two boys and a girl. In 1960, the same year Richard died, Masil's boys, age ten and seven, were playing in a wheat field on their ranch in Oregon. They discovered a box they thought contained gold, but it contained dynamite caps. The box blew up, killing the ten year old and blinding the seven year old.

Masil was a nurse and took care of her son in the hospital, only leaving his side to attend the funeral of her other son. The doctors told her not to cry and to keep her injured son from crying. They were hoping to save his sight, but failed. As a result of these demands, Masil did not have the opportunity to grieve or to deal with her feelings. She ended up with a severe health challenge herself. The circumstances of Masil's life in relationship to her children were very similar to mine She had a son who died the same year as my son, a handicapped son, and a younger daughter Colleen's age who is just fine.

Shortly after the boys' traumatic accident, Masil developed non-tropical sprue, an allergy to all forms of gluten, including wheat, oats, barley, rye. If she ate even a bite of anything that contained gluten, she would suffer uncontrollable diarrhea; this went on for several years until Masil met Ione and her husband Asa when they moved to Dufur, Oregon. Asa was the new minister of the Christian Church, Disciples of Christ where Masil and her husband attended church.

Because Ione had an extensive background in psychology, she was actively involved in counseling and other activities in the church. During counseling sessions with Masil, Ione was able to lead her back to the time of the accident and to help her experience and then release the feelings of grief she had buried and left unexpressed for so many years, feelings that her body expressed for her through the illness. The body-mind connection was clear. The boys were killed in a wheat field; Masil's illness took the form of an allergy to wheat.

Once Masil's emotions were expressed and dealt with, Ione and Masil proceeded to the next step: healing the "incurable" disease. The sprue was diagnosed at the Oregon Health Science Center in Portland, and

Masil's doctors had made it very clear that she would have to live with this condition for the rest of her life. However, Masil and Ione believed that God can do anything, can cure anything. Masil had done her inner work; now it was time for the healing. The two women fasted and prayed for three days, then went to a quiet place in the woods. Ione laid hands on Masil's stomach; they both visualized Masil's intestinal tract functioning perfectly; then, they gave thanks to God for the healing. Masil's stomach began to undulate under Ione's hand, and Masil had an inner knowing that she was healed. She went home and ate a hamburger bun and a donut, with no ill effects. Several years after the healing, Masil's intestinal tract remains totally healthy.

After this miracle, Ione and Masil began a prayer and healing ministry, and miracle healings for others followed. Eventually, they were led to northern Idaho to continue their work. They formed the Holo Center, a non-profit organization dedicated to the integration of body-mind-spirit. We found it interesting that Masil as nurse reflects body; Ione as psychologist reflects mind; I as minister reflect spirit. Of course, the goal is for everyone to integrate and harmoniously express all three aspects.

After the stress and pressure of the ministry in Coeur d'Alene, I gratefully settled down to life at the Holo Center where there was unlimited quiet time, - time to rest, to reflect, to heal. There was still a part of me that felt torn, wounded and confused regarding Unity, that wondered if I should go back to Unity Village headquarters and try to straighten things out. However, another part of me recognized the need for personal healing, for time and space to gain a perspective on it all.

With this unlimited time and love and support from Ione and Masil, I began to learn and absorb new healing methods, to pass this learning along to others in counseling, and to benefit greatly from these new methods myself. Rebirthing, inner healing, working with my inner child, dream work and sub-personality investigation all proved to be methods of great value. These healing techniques, as well as constant love and support, began to bring to light and then dissipate the pockets of self-loathing I'd tucked away in the dark corners of my psyche. Regular meditation had been extremely beneficial and had laid a foundation of strength and courage which empowered me to truly and honestly look at myself. By the grace of God, I was provided with the methods and the time and space to do the necessary deeper inner healing.

For so much of my life, I'd been busy dealing with crisis events and crisis people. If I found time or space to be alone, I usually felt lonely, which drove me to fill up available solitary time and space with people and projects. Although I always helped myself by using the books and ideas available to me, they could only take me so far. Certainly, the cosmic philosophy I had learned through transcendental meditation and the Unity philosophy with its practical approach helped immensely, but there was still something missing. All too often, the void was still there.

In the space and time at the Center, I was experiencing unconditional love and nurturing. At the same time I was learning and applying incredibly effective psychological and spiritual methods of healing. I felt no pressure to be looking for someone or something to "fill the void." At the Center there was companionship, love, laughter. There was no pressure to earn my keep. I did what I could, and that was enough. I slept as many hours of the day as I needed to sleep. Life was easy and laid back.

I began to work seriously with my dreams, which included the concept of the anima/animus. Carl Jung taught about the male component in every female (animus) and the female component in every male (anima) People look "out there" for the unacknowledged opposite part of themselves. People must get to know and claim all their aspects so as to allow the balance of male and female within to come together in an inner marriage. Then, people are balanced and whole, not needing to seek fulfillment only through opposite sex partners, and they are thus much better equipped to enter into healthy relationships. About this time, I began to have recurring dreams of being a new bride about to marry Duane. I saw that Duane symbolized my masculine self and that the dreams were depicting the emerging balance and integration of my male and female energies as a marriage

During all the years I was married to Duane, I wanted him to be a perfect husband and to be "respectable." I wanted him to command and then bestow upon me the same kind of community respect that I had wanted my dad to reflect for me. Neither Duane nor my dad could do this because of their alcoholism. I now began to understand that I had wanted both of these men to do for me what I could ultimately only do for myself. Respect is an inside job.

With Ione and Masil's steady guidance and love, I continued to review my life and to heal past wounds, starting with the womb experience. I learned that while in the womb, babies absorb the mother's emotions. Ruth, my birth mother, must have been very upset and frightened, having been sent away and rejected because of her pregnancy. For as long as I could remember, feelings of shame, unworthiness, "not good enough" had been almost impossible for me to dissipate. Now, at least, I began to understand their probable originating point, the womb

In the process of inner healing, the adult Julie loved and cared about Ruth and the baby Julie, starting with the womb experience. Ione and Masil taught me to see Jesus (representing father love) and Mary (representing mother love) blessing me in the womb and through the process of birth, and then, continuing the inner healing process, through all the ages and stages of my life. While in a relaxed state, I was guided to remember and to heal the difficult memories and to bless the good ones. Because in Spirit, in God, there is no time or space, it was possible for me to go back and bring love, understanding, and the healing power of God into every event and circumstance of my life. Many years ago this process was called "healing of the memories," but later became known as "inner healing."

Closely related to this is "inner child work." The child we were continues to live within us and to influence our lives. Little Julie May desperately needed love and stability and went after it the only way she knew: by searching for the right and perfect man to take care of her, just as she had been taught in those early soap operas and fairy tales. Of course, the society of the 40's and 50's assumed that a woman needed a man to be whole. Under the circumstances, it was not easy to see the truth, to unlearn the easily accepted lie.

I facilitated my inner child's healing by 1) loving little Julie May, 2) by teaching her that I will never leave or abandon her, 3) by helping her to release her pain and shame, 4) by teaching her that God loves her and will always be with her no matter what. I discovered that Julie May's pain and dysfunction have been the catalyst for much of my unskillful behavior as an adult. I saw that acknowledging, loving, and teaching little Julie May was going to be a lifelong process. Nonetheless, as I owned and healed more and more of myself, I was allowing more of the energy that is truly ME to be expressed. As I was legitimizing myself, I began to understand that God has no illegitimate children! The light of truth was transforming my pain and suffering and teaching me that I am an indestructible spiritual being who has never been outside the love of God. I saw that I had been instructed, guided, and protected in many ways during past difficult times. Even when I felt most alone, I was not.

The continuing inner healing process included spending great amounts of time dealing with the people who had "wronged" me in the past, such as my dad, grandfather, and uncle. My purpose was to see from a cosmic perspective. Because I chose or attracted every person and event into my life to learn the lesson of love, I searched for ways they had taught me about love. I discovered that it is never too late to learn from a person or a situation. My task was to stop resenting, to stop being a victim, to further release the negativity from the past and to live in love in the present moment. I had previously made some progress because I had willed to forgive. I knew that not forgiving is poisonous, and I asked for help from my Christ Self, my Higher Self, that I might totally forgive and be free. However, I found that just when I believed I was finally free of all resentment, another layer of it would surface, making another round of forgiveness necessary. Because there was more leisure time at the Center, there was more opportunity for stored negatives to surface, more challenge to heal and forgive.

I thought about Dad, Grandpa Perry, and Uncle Conrad and how their sexual molestation hurt me, how I carried a deep sense of shame over it, and I wondered how they could have treated me as something they could use. How could they not care about how it might affect me? And the answers came back: Because of their disease of pedophilia, they couldn't stop themselves. Because they didn't understand the damage they were doing. And then I asked myself, "If my soul chose these experiences, why did I choose them?" Because I was a molester in a former life and want to balance karma? Because I need to understand that I am a beautiful child of God no matter what someone does to my body? Because I need to learn to forgive? To have compassion for everyone, including molesters? Perhaps all of the above.

As I released more and more pain and resentment, I began to acknowledge the kindness and good nature of my dad and Grandpa Perry. What they did was wrong; child molestation can never be condoned. The behavior must be prevented and stopped. Yet, it was healing to separate the act from the actor, to acknowledge the worth and value of those, who out of their own ignorance and pain, have injured me. I knew that I could only hurt myself by staying stuck in the past; therefore, I eagerly embraced this more cosmic perspective.

I thought about Duane and the misery he inflicted upon himself over the years. I had understood for a very long time that he had never deliberately set out to hurt me, that I had been totally unrealistic in my expectations of him. What could be the cosmic lesson with him? Did I (as Ruth Rebe suggested in her past life reading) treat him with little respect and consideration in a former life? Did I attempt to balance my karma with him this time? Did I need to learn my own worth and value and not expect to get it from a mate or anyone else? Did I need to learn to forgive and love him no matter what? I felt the answer to be "yes" to all these questions. I blessed Duane yet again and released him to his highest good.

I saw that Ted, Buck, Tom, Joe and other men I'd drawn into my life all helped me understand the necessity of taking responsibility for myself. I wanted each of them to fix my life, to play the role of Prince Charming. They each taught me in some way that I must be responsible for myself. The Unity organization and the church in Coeur d' Alene did not bear the responsibility for making my life work either. It took a few years of continuing inner work before it became clear to me that I'd placed some of the same unrealistic expectations upon these organizations that I'd placed upon the men in my life. It still is a difficult challenge to take one hundred percent responsibility for my own life and to trust God one hundred percent of the time to unfold the events of my life in Divine Order!

At that time an abundance of literature began to be published around the issue of co-dependency. I began to understand that I fit the description. It was helpful to recognize that my early life situations and my feelings and behavior as an adult were not that uncommon. I saw my unhealthy patterns and what action I needed to take to be healed. It was a great comfort to have a better grasp of the problem, to have some methods to solve the problem, and to have a clear idea of what I wanted to accomplish. I wanted to move away from co-dependency. I wanted to become empowered.

I learned that a Co-dependent person 1) is often the victim of sexual, physical, emotional abuse 2) never feels good enough, is desperate to be "normal." 3) fears the past 4) is sure that being happy depends on other people 5) is compelled to prove his or her worth 6) is constantly looking for something missing or lacking 7) can't set boundaries and is not clear about own rights 8) may have sexual problems, eating disorders, alcohol or drug problems.

I was determined to become an Empowered person who 1) puts the healthy adult ego in charge 2) uses the past to learn and grow 3) knows true identity as a child of God 4) realistically looks at strengths and weaknesses, feels neither superior or inferior to anyone else. 5) has the courage to be unpopular if need be. 6) knows that each soul is responsible for its own choices. 7) has the courage to look within, does not deny or repress. 8) is always open and receptive to new things, but is not driven to fill an inner void - knows there is a higher power and acknowledges it.

I diligently continued to work toward my goal, but discovered to my chagrin that dealing with past shame, anger and nonforgiveness was not a quick one time procedure. It was a matter of handling the layers and memories as they came up. For example, after I thought I'd totally forgiven my dad, more hurt and angry feelings continued to arise. Time to call in the Christ and forgive again! This was true with many people and circumstances. It seemed that once I had the will and the clear time to focus on my healing, things continually came up, things I'd long since buried and consciously forgotten. It was important to understand this as a natural process. I was not regressing! There were merely many levels and layers of memories and emotions to deal with.

Another helpful and life-changing discovery for me was that each of us has many facets or sub-personalities. Sometimes they work in harmony with each other. Sometimes they don't. We consciously live out of some of these aspects, while at the same time, other facets and sub-personalities remain unconscious, unknown to us. Some of our sub-personalities are more productive and life-enhancing than others. The field of Psycho-Synthesis, pioneered by Italian psychiatrist Roberto Assagioli seeks to help people get in touch with, heal, and integrate their many sub-personalities. These personalities are like the different numbers on the Wheel of Fortune, and we focus upon different ones at different times. In the center of the wheel, the very core of our Being, is our Christ Self, our Higher Self, our Divine Self. To the degree that we are "poised and centered in the Christ Mind," the subpersonalities around the wheel can be recognized, healed, and integrated to serve the Higher purpose. To the degree that we allow ourselves to be "caught in the drama," stirred up by the unhealed parts of ourselves, we suffer and learn the hard way.

We star in our own unpredictable soap opera. I had often been torn and pulled in different directions, in conflict with myself. Many times I had been dismayed and shocked at my angry vengeful thoughts or impulsive actions. Getting to know and understand the inner cast of characters who vie for leading roles on the stage where my life is playing itself out was very useful. So often the martyr and the victim have had leading roles. I was determined to educate these parts of myself, to teach them that the soul expressing through the personality of Julie in this lifetime has chosen every experience for the good purpose of learning the lesson of unconditional love for all, including myself

I was able to see the lessons of love and forgiveness in my relationships and marriages. The victim and the martyr willingly claimed less and less focus and energy and agreed to become bit players instead of major characters. As I became more aware of the need to have mercy and compassion for myself and others, I had the courage to more thoroughly examine my own weaknesses and mistakes and to take responsibility for them. I discovered that it is never too late to learn from an event in my life, no matter how long ago it may have occurred.

At the same time, I allowed the fun loving clown who lives within me more time in the spotlight and noticed that the laughter the clown generates is a powerful healing force. Ione, Masil, and I began to sing melodramatic operas to each other about problem people and situations in our lives, which released anger and stress and helped put our grievances into a more rational perspective. I was actually coming to a place where I could make jokes about all the men who had been in my life. One evening, our neighbor, Joy, was visiting us when the phone rang. Lucretia, who was also staying at the center for a few months of healing work, answered the phone. Joy's husband wanted to speak to Joy, but Lucretia thought she heard him asking for Julie. "May I tell her who's calling?" Lucretia asked. "Tell her that her husband is calling," he answered. Lucretia was puzzled and asked, "Which one?"

Naturally, Joy's husband was becoming terribly confused because he, as far as he knew, was Joy's only husband. After a little more conversation, Lucretia finally understood that he wanted to speak to his wife, JOY. This whole scenario struck us all as incredibly funny, and we enjoyed a prolonged period of hysterical laughter. Researchers have found that humor is healing for both the mind and body, and I believe it! This incident of prolonged laughter over my marriages burned out more of the residue of pain and shame that insisted on hanging around.

During that time my dear friend Helice, fellow ministerial student and master mind partner, was in a very successful ministry in Oakton, Virginia. She was getting ready to take a group on a tour of Greece, Egypt, and Israel. Masil, Ione, and I arranged to go along on this dream trip. The Mediterranean area has always fascinated me. If there is anything to the idea of reincarnation, I know I've been at home in these places. The tour included a three day cruise of the Greek islands, including Patmos where John is reported to have written the book of Revelation. It was October, the perfect time of year. Helice celebrated her birthday in Greece; Ione celebrated her birthday a few days later in Egypt. Words could never adequately describe the joy of being in these places. I felt like I was floating in a bubble of ecstasy most of the time

On the island tour, our ship stopped on the coast of Turkey, and we walked through the ruins of what used to be Ephesus. As the guide was pointing out the beauty of the intricate tile work on the walkway, I looked down at the tile. From somewhere deep within a deep sob came to the surface, a sob of joy and recognition. One part of me just observed; another part was totally surprised at what was happening.

This was totally unexpected in this particular place. I would not have been surprised if I had experienced a sense of recognition at the pyramids or the acropolis in Athens, but here I was totally amazed. Not only was I amazed at the location, but I am amazed that the experience was so emotional, so obviously a past life recognition. Things like that didn't normally happen to me. That we perhaps carry a thread of remembrance along with us from lifetime to lifetime had been a bit of information in my head, but to have such a deep emotional experience was a thrill, even though it lasted only briefly.

Back in Idaho, Ione and I began to dream about seeing more of the world. There wasn't enough activity at the Center to keep all three of us busy and supported. Masil was a few years older and enjoyed working at the Center; she would be happy to keep the home fires burning if we could find a way to extend our ministry through travel. We had been offering workshops at the Center, so we decided to put several workshops together and offer them to some Unity churches.

Ione has an impressive background. She studied Gestalt Therapy with Fritz Perls and Reality Therapy with William Glasser and was in groups with Ruth Carter Stapleton as Ruth was developing a unique inner healing process. She has studied dreams for many years and is an excellent dream therapist. We began to see that we could work together, each offering our unique talents. Ione convinced me that as I share my wounds and my struggle to heal them, that people will be encouraged to begin and then stay with their own healing process. I made a commitment to be more open and vulnerable, more personal in our workshop ministry.

I phoned several minister friends and managed to set up a six week tour of Midwest Unity churches. We were gratified by the response of the ministers and participants. We saw that we had areas to improve and fine tune, but that we could do it! Ione and I were excited about traveling and meeting new people. We both married young and had children right away; back in the sixties when many young people were having all kinds of adventures, we were in the midst of wife and mother responsibilities. Now it was our turn to have some fun and adventure, to be middle-aged hippies! We trusted that God would open the appropriate doors for us and close the inappropriate ones as we sought opportunities to share our talents. We were ready to let the adventures begin!

CHAPTER ELEVEN
THE UNFINISHED SYMPHONY

"There are many gates to the sacred,
and they are as wide as we need them to be."
- Anderson & Hopkins

Ione and I enthusiastically developed several workshops designed to help others in their healing process. Subjects included dealing with grief and guilt, working toward healthier relationships, understanding the body-mind-spirit connection, and what turned out to be our most popular offering, working with dreams. Because Ione was a dream therapist, we had reaped many benefits from working with our own dreams. We had fun creating a practical workshop that would motivate others to take their dreams seriously. At the Center, Ione, Masil and I had often sat over morning coffee discussing our dreams and possible interpretations. These sessions facilitated an ever expanding awareness of the hidden elements of our psyches and how much these hidden elements influenced what we saw as reality.

Dreams often reveal what we don't consciously know about ourselves and show us where healing is needed. Furthermore, dreams quite often have a universal message which not only reaches out to the dreamer, but to others as well. Right in the midst of planning the dream workshop and feeling confident that my healing was almost complete, I had the following dream, which taught me otherwise. It gave me a strong personal message but included a universal message for others as well.

My dream: I am slowly walking through a hospital filled with many patients. People in various stages of recovery are lying or sitting on hospital beds on each side of a central corridor. I realize that it is important to send out energy of love and light to these people as I walk in their midst. I keep walking toward a door in the back, open it and find myself in a back ward filled with dark, threatening, and very ugly people. They are behind bars in jail cells, their hands are reaching out to me, clutching at my clothing, pleading for my help. Terrified and repulsed, I pull away from them and scream for help. The screams awaken me.

Heart pounding, body shaking, I sat up in bed and knew that this was a dream I could not ignore. One effective way to unlock a dream's meaning is to look at everyone and everything in it as a part of ourselves. This dream seemed to be telling me I was in a space of healing (the hospital) and many parts of me were in a state of recovery; I was acknowledging and blessing them and their progress. However, there were parts of me hidden in the back ward (unconscious mind) because they were too repulsive to deal with. These parts were reaching out for help, but I felt too frightened to acknowledge them. This dream was telling me I was not finished with healing work. There were things I hadn't been able to bring myself to look at and deal with - and I was scared to death of them! I felt very humbled, and then awed by the magnitude of the work that was still obviously necessary.

After a few minutes, I went back into the dream using meditative visualization, a process of recreating the dream in the mind while awake. But, I did not go back into the dream alone. I brought along a Light Being, a spiritual guide and protector, my elder brother and way shower, Jesus the Christ. Together, we went back into the hospital, walked down the corridor, and blessed the people in the front ward. We approached the back ward door and walked through; because the light of the Christ protected me, I felt no fear, no impulse to run away. Together we reached out to the dark figures, filling them with light, love, and compassion, and they soaked it up. Then Jesus the Christ and I walked back through the hospital to the front steps. He opened his arms, and as we embraced, a clear message moved through my mind and heart: "Julie my dear precious child, there is nothing you have done or nothing within you that is so shameful that it is beyond My love and healing power! There is no need to hide from yourself; you are worthy; allow yourself to be healed."

Tears streaming down my cheeks, I came to a new level of awareness, a new level of self-acceptance and hope. This turning point in my growth gave me the strength and courage to look deeper within myself and the wisdom to understand that more healing was necessary and possible. I believe this was also a universal message: In spite of our fear, we can trust the power of the loving Christ to guide and to heal; there is nothing inside anyone that is beyond redemption.

Many people with whom we worked in counseling and workshops confessed they were terrified that deep within themselves something inherently ugly and bad resides, making them basically unworthy. So much of my ministry has turned out to be simply sharing my story and what works for me. It was very comforting for many, including myself, to realize that our struggle to become whole was very common and much like everyone else's struggle to become whole.

Another workshop, Changes and Transitions, helped people deal with loss and grief, and also turned out to be as healing for me as it was for others. During the course of the workshop, I naturally talked about the death of Richard and how I delayed and resisted the grief process. At the time Richard died, neither I nor the people around me understood the vital importance of honestly facing feelings of grief and guilt. As a result, these feelings remained unresolved. This is an all too common circumstance when people lose someone close to them. Our purpose in the workshops was to help people understand the dynamics of the grief process and to offer tools and techniques for continued use on their own.

One particular workshop exercise encouraged people to see a departed loved one standing in front of them, to talk to that loved one about any guilt, and to ask forgiveness. On the other hand, if a departed loved one had done something to the participant that needed forgiveness, they confronted that loved one and then offered forgiveness. This was known as finishing business, releasing everyone to go on to their highest good. I always led this exercise, and as I led it, I called Richard to me and asked for his forgiveness.

One incident and the guilt around it had been particularly painful for me. During the summer trip when I left Duane and traveled to Texas with Richard when he was two years old, he spilled his orange soda in the car. Because the car had no air conditioning, we were both hot and tired. Losing control, I had screamed at him and slapped him. I cringed at the memory of it, remorseful over having done such a thing. Consequently, in this visualization, I asked for his forgiveness. No matter that I had done this very same visualization many times. I continued to feel guilt in spite of the fact that Richard always smiled and assured me, "I love you Mom, I do forgive you." Then I would feel much better, for awhile anyway. However, every time I led others in the visualization, the orange soda incident kept presenting itself to me. One evening, the exercise took a new turn. I was into it and asking Richard to forgive me, but instead of his usual response, he put his hands on his hips, rolled his eyes back and said, "Mom, will you get off it! Of course I've forgiven you - I love you!" As a result, I never had the need to deal with that incident again. I finally felt forgiven. This experience reminded me yet again that working with our issues is a process; layers continue to peel off until the business is finished. Indeed, we sometimes have huge breakthroughs, but more often it's a process of taking one small step after another until we know we're finished with something. Sometimes what seems like a big breakthrough helps us to see and work with the many small steps that need to follow.

My hospital dream was a breakthrough experience because it helped me to recognize the presence of the shadows and their desire to be healed. However, because it took years and perhaps lifetimes to accumulate all the pain and shame, cleaning it up is an ongoing process that takes as long as it takes. I'd often tried to skip over the inner psychological work because I was in a rush to be more "spiritual." I eventually discovered that psychological healing IS also spiritual healing. On the other hand, I discovered that I could not work solely on the psychological level and expect ultimate fulfillment. Without the spiritual element I ran into a dead end of frustration. I finally realized there is no separation between spirituality, psychology, science, art, life. I learned that it's useful to embrace it all and to appreciate what each has to offer.

My experiences with Richard were a blend of psychological and spiritual healing. Richard visited me often in dreams and came to me in a dream shortly after his death to assure me that he was fine and to instruct me to take care of Robert and Colleen. Over the years I dreamed of him often and felt comforted, as if we'd had a visit with each other. The dreams continued throughout the period we were teaching and learning about "finishing business" in the workshops. Richard was always nine years old in the dreams, his age when he made his transition. But now, I had a dream of him as a young man. No action or words, just a close-up of Richard's face. He had the same sandy hair and happy blue eyes, the same warm and loving smile.

Reviewing the dream, I concluded it was showing me I had indeed finished my grief work and emotionally released Richard to continue on his journey, although I knew our loving connection would always exist. This interpretation felt right and good. Yet, there was just one small piece of unfinished business that I couldn't quite let go of - foolish and impossible as it seemed - I wanted a real physical hug. I trusted I would receive this kind of satisfying embrace from Richard after I made my own transition, but my mother's heart couldn't stop yearning for a more tangible connection.

About two weeks after I dreamed of Richard as an adult, Ione and I were at a Unity church in Vancouver, Washington presenting a Saturday morning dream workshop. A sign outside the church invited passersby to join us. A few minutes into the workshop, a young man walked in, and we made room for him in our circle. He looked quite familiar, and I searched my mind for why. Then it hit me. A chill crept down my back, and I began to feel very strange, as if I were in a waking dream witnessing the whole scene from afar. The young man looked just like Richard looked in the dream!

At break time I approached him and attempted to explain that he was a grown up version of my son. With a friendly smile, he listened attentively to what I was saying. His essence felt very much like Richard's sweet essence. Because of some problems with his own mother, this young man was happy to receive and soak up some attention and hugs from me. He had never been in the church before; he just happened to see the sign and make a quick decision to come into the church and too see what the workshop was all about. As we were packing up and getting ready to leave, I was still trying to assimilate what had just happened. How could Richard in the dream and the young man at the workshop be so alike? "Very strange," I thought. I talked to Ione about all this and she reminded me about the date: July 26th, Richard's birthday! Had I received a birthday hug from Richard on his birthday? I realized Richard had once more found a way to say "Hey Mom, I'm alright and I love you!"

As we covered the miles on our workshop tours, Ione and I naturally spent much time together. Two creative and strong people with our own ideas, we were challenged to learn lessons in cooperation and understanding, and these lessons pushed our growing edge. However, we worked very well together most of the time, and we respected each other for being willing to look honestly at our motivations and actions. When we did clash, it was little Earle Ione and little Julie May who had the difficulty. We challenged ourselves to not only deal with our own unhealed areas but to have compassion for the other as well. The result was that we worked with our own inner child and learned to love and understand the inner child of the other. This in turn enhanced our work with others in the Relationship workshops because we presented examples of problems and the solving of them which we'd drawn from our own experience. We, as well as people attending the workshops, dealt with the same basic challenge of loving and accepting ourselves and then loving and accepting each other.

As Ione and I further investigated our interactions with each other, we continually made new discoveries. What bugged me also bugged Ione. We didn't like to be accused; we wanted to be appreciated; we wanted to receive some grace when we make mistakes. When a mistake of Ione's bugged me, I soon made the same or a similar error and experienced how it felt to be the guilty one. Ione remembered one of her grandmother's sayings: "It depends on whose ox is in the ditch!" We began to have more sympathy for the ox of the other, and to take things less seriously. Living in an ongoing workshop, we were grateful for a component of humor.

In the beginning, we traveled in a small station wagon packed with workshop materials, food and cooking supplies, and personal items. There was not an inch to spare. Sometimes we stayed with friends or relatives, sometimes at a Motel 6, sometimes with people at the church where we were doing a workshop, sometimes with the minister of the church. I had several Unity friends and classmates around the country who usually invited us to be their guests when we were in their area. I was delighted to get to know these people at a much deeper level than had been possible in a school setting. Out in a ministry, there is often no one for the minister to share with on a more personal level. Ione and I found ourselves being friend and counselor to ministers and felt privileged this was so. Many eventually came to the Holo Center for intensive retreats where we were able to love and pamper, to counsel and pray with these dedicated people who give so much to everyone else. The gift I received from the ministers in return was an understanding that my problems in the Coeur d' Alene church were not unusual. Other ministers shared similar devastating experiences, which helped me to fit my own experience into a broader perspective.

During the months we traveled in the station wagon, Ione and I began to look at motor homes and to dream of owning one. When we passed RV sale lots, we stopped, looked, and dreamed. Eventually, in a lot in Beaverton, Oregon we found a new 21 foot Coachman we liked. The dealership was running a "too good to pass up" sale, offering several thousand dollars off the original purchase price. We decided to take the plunge. Neither of us had driven a motor home before, so we learned by doing. We picked our new vehicle up at rush hour, and I volunteered to be the first driver. Luckily, we managed to arrive at our nearby destination without mishap, but later, we had a few embarrassing experiences. At a California dealership where we stopped for a minor adjustment, I backed into a chain link fence and knocked out a tail light. I had a lollipop in my mouth at the time and wondered if the mechanic thought a child was driving the rig! While visiting Colleen, in the process of backing up our RV as close to the garage as possible, I ran into the rain gutter, bending it and punching a nail hole through our back bathroom. It definitely took awhile to get used to the dimensions of the thing. We had learned the first week that the vehicle was slightly wider in the back than in the front. Ione, or was it me, I can't remember for sure, drove too close to a curb and crushed the rear hub cap.

On the freeways, wind gusts were a tremendous challenge. In the wide open spaces in the west, we held the wheel in an iron grip, at times fearing we'd be blown off the road. At the end of the day when it was time to park and hook up, other challenges arose. We needed to make sure all the cords, hoses, and pipes were properly attached, especially the sewer pipe. We did a commendable job with this on most of our travels. However, we once failed to get the sewer hose secured tightly enough; we never made that mistake again! Needless to say, it was very unpleasant work cleaning up the mess, and very embarrassing besides with an RV parked close by on each side.

Quite often, we parked in churchyards. Usually, this was a pleasant experience which provided serene surroundings and our own private space with convenient access to the churches. However, when we worked in an inner city church, it didn't feel comfortable to be in the church parking lot overnight, so we stayed with people from the congregation or found a mobile home park nearby. Sometimes it was a borderline situation. The Unity church in Everett, Washington was borderline, close to downtown with some rather shabby apartments on one side, but the neighborhood seemed safe enough. The minister arranged for us to park behind the church and to plug into electricity. On that Saturday night, we settled in early to be ready for the church services and workshop on Sunday morning. In the middle of the night we awakened to the sound of gun shots and police sirens. We had no idea what was going on out there, but we knew we'd better surround the vehicle with light and double check the doors. We gave thanks to God when it was all over. The next day we read about the police shoot-out with a robbery suspect. After the workshop we moved to a mobile home park outside town.

Another trying situation arose in Charleston, South Carolina while we were parked on a busy downtown street in front of the Unity church. We intended to park there during our workshop presentation only, then drive back to our space in the RV park outside of town. Just as we were locking up the vehicle and getting ready to go into the church for the workshop, the mechanism of the door jammed, and it refused to lock. It was nearly time for our workshop to begin, people were waiting for us, and we had to get on with it. After several desperate and unsuccessful efforts to fix the door, we tied it shut with a long shoestring, surrounded everything with light, and trusted. We were grateful to find our home just as we left it when we came out after the workshop.

As we continued to travel the highways and byways from the west coast to the east coast, from Florida to New York and many points in between, we were surprised to see so many recreational vehicles. It looked like a large proportion of the American people were on the road! Parks were everywhere, and with the help of our trusty Woodhalls directory, we had no problem finding the facilities we needed. We tried to make productive use of our driving time. We critiqued and planned workshops, read books to each other, sorted out our lives. We also sang a lot and just enjoyed the beauty of the countryside. Sometimes when we had a sleepy attack at the same time and felt like a danger on the road, we drove into the parking lot of a supermarket or a McDonald's, pulled out the bed and took a short nap. Managing to find a way to get our needs met, we felt like "queens of the road," at home anywhere.

We made it a point to spend some time in Michigan and Texas with my friends and relatives and time in Iowa and Oregon with Ione's friends and relatives. Mom was having continuing heart problems but survived heart by-pass surgery when she was nearly eighty. We counseled and prayed with her and gave her lots of love and attention. An incredibly strong lady, she made it through that challenge and many that came after. Robert and Lee Ann continued to do remarkably well, with Robert staying at home and Lee Ann going outside the home to work. Robert sometimes felt life had cheated him, but I was thankful he was able to be married, to live in a comfortable home, and to be free of institutional restraints. It was so much more than I was encouraged to hope for in earlier years.

For many years, I'd had a dream. I wanted to be not only the mother of the bride at my daughter's wedding, I wanted to be the minister as well. This dream was about to come true, but with a few challenges thrown in. Colleen decided to be married in Clare, Michigan in June, to have her father walk her down the aisle, to have her sisters be bridesmaids, and to have me perform the wedding ceremony. I felt I had cleared and released any painful emotions about Duane and Phyllis, and I was happy to go along with Colleen's plans. I had the same loving feelings toward Duane that I'd had for years, yet at the same time, I totally acknowledged his union with Phyllis. I believed the love I felt toward Duane was on a soul level beyond any human attachment.

We met together on Friday evening for the rehearsal: the bride and groom, Duane and Phyllis, Colleen's four sisters, and for a reason unknown to me, Phyllis' parents, the Browns were there. The remainder of the wedding party would be at the service the next day. When I saw Phyllis' parents, I was shocked by the burst of anger that rose up within me, but I quickly recognized the reason. These people had long been alcoholics. After I was able to stop blaming Duane and Phyllis for ruining my life, I felt empathy for Phyllis because both her parents were usually in the bar. However, I didn't feel any personal animosity toward her parents until one evening shortly after Colleen went to live with Duane and Phyllis.

They had gone away and left Phyllis' mother in charge of the house. Colleen was out on a date, and when she came home, Mrs. Brown was drunk and started verbally abusing Colleen: "You're a no good slut just like your no good slut mother! You're disgusting!" Colleen called me in tears. At ten o'clock that night I drove fifty miles to Clare, picked Colleen up, and brought her back to Big Rapids. When I saw this woman at the rehearsal, I remembered what she had said to Colleen and felt an explosion of anger. However, I couldn't allow myself to show those feelings. It is a relief when the rehearsal was completed without any unpleasantness.

Ione and I were staying with Mom in St. Louis, just a few miles south of Clare. The next morning we walked to the park near Mom's house, where Ione helped me deal with my chaotic emotions. There were no people in the park that morning, so it was safe to cry and scream. I thought everything had been cleared and healed concerning Duane and Phyllis, but it was obvious this was not quite so. The situation presented me the opportunity to finish some business, just what we'd been teaching others to do.

First, I looked at my anger toward Mrs. Brown and saw that my anger came from her judgment of me. She mirrored - reflected back to me - a part of myself that judged myself, that agreed with the names she called me. What I really needed was forgiveness, mercy and compassion towards myself. If I totally loved myself, it wouldn't matter what anyone else called me or thought about me. The anger released when I took responsibility for my own reactions and emotions. Continuing the process, I acknowledged Phyllis and her parents as fellow souls, learning their lessons, playing their parts in life, just as we all are. I saw us standing together with Jesus the Christ, light and love flowing from his heart and surrounding us all.

Finally, I realized that although I continued to love Duane, it was appropriate to further release him as he continued on his chosen path with Phyllis. I affirmed and acknowledged, "The Light of the Christ is now establishing harmony, love, and order in tomorrow's wedding activities. All is well. I choose to walk in love, to see from the cosmic viewpoint." The next day the wedding went very smoothly. Colleen was a beautiful bride, and everything unfolded just as she had pictured it would, just as I had dreamed it would. The reception was held in Duane and Phyllis' home. Phyllis was gracious. Roy and Ollie told me that I had conducted a beautiful ceremony, and I felt the unspoken love between us. Phyllis reminded everyone that she and Duane had celebrated their 25th anniversary the month before. By the grace of God, I was able to congratulate them and mean it. With God, all things are possible!

In January 1988, we made a working trip to Hawaii. Ione and I had been traveling a good portion of the last four years, so we were happy to be taking a break in one of our favorite places. We'd left the RV in California and were house sitting and doing some workshops during this six week stay in paradise. Walking along the street in Honolulu one afternoon, Ione and I paused to allow a slow moving car coming out of a parking garage to cross in front of us. I glanced at the driver. It looked like Joe. It was Joe! "Joe?" I walked over to the car. "Julie, is that YOU?" he asked. Cars were waiting behind him, so he parked the car and met us at the restaurant just up the street. Over tea, we caught up. He was definitely happily married, but seemed very happy to have this opportunity to chat. I, too, felt very good about this chance to touch base, to finish business. We both had come to the conclusion that we could have acted in a better way during our brief marriage, that if we had been able to compromise, we probably could have made the marriage work. It felt good to hold hands and look each other in the eye and acknowledge this. After about an hour, we lovingly wished each other well and went on our way, appreciating the opportunity to say good-bye properly. Perhaps because we genuinely loved each other, we wanted to believe our marriage might have survived.

Yet, being honest with myself, I knew that all the unhealed parts of myself, if left unhealed, would probably have sabotaged our life together anyway. As I looked back from a more healed space within myself, I knew I didn't do better because I didn't know better. However, everything happened just the way it needed to happen. I was now learning to go forward, to bless the past, to let the regrets go. In this way, I gave myself space to joyfully embrace the present.

As Ione and I continued to relax and enjoy Hawaii, I saw from the Unity minister's letter announcing church vacancies, that the church on the north shore of Oahu was looking for a minister. All the residue of the unfinished business I had pushed aside concerning the Unity ministry rose up within me. The intensity of my desire to put the church issue to rest by trying to once again minister in a permanent church setting propelled me to make a phone call to Unity. I arranged a meeting with the committee that could decide whether or not I might be reinstated and accept a position as minister in a Unity church. With Ione's blessing and support, I decided to visit the Unity church on the north shore and inquire about the opening.

I was invited to guest speak and to have an interview with the board. They agreed to take an application later if or when I could officially send them one. I was excited about the possibility of proving myself capable of managing a church ministry without problems and turmoil. In spite of elapsed time and increased perspective, I was still carrying a degree of guilt and shame about my problems in the Coeur d'Alene church. I knew I would never allow myself to get drawn into a nasty church conflict again. I would resign if anything like that would even begin to happen. I had a pleasant experience speaking at the church and talking with the board, but I recognized that they had challenges I probably would find difficult to handle. I realized that this ministry wasn't the right one for me at that time.

Back in California on the day of my meeting with the Unity committee, I was fighting off flu and chills, but managed to medicate myself enough to tough it out. The meeting was amiable; I felt listened to; I pointed out that I'd learned much and would never again become involved in a church split. Because of the workshops, the committee was satisfied I'd been actively involved in Unity, and so they made the determination to reinstate me. I was free to have my resume sent to wherever I wanted. As I looked over the newsletter, I saw that Tallahassee, Florida was open. Ione and I remembered our very pleasant experience there about a year earlier. We remembered the beautiful wooded setting, the feeling in the sanctuary, and the warm hospitality of the minister and the congregation. It seemed a perfect place to send my resume.

A prompt invitation from Unity of Tallahassee to speak and to interview followed. It seemed many people had a pleasant memory of our being there. I flew out to Tallahassee for a few days, and Ione stayed in the motor home near the ocean south of San Francisco. It was March. The talk at church, the board interview, the visitation with other leaders went very smoothly. The board met in special session on Sunday evening, and I was offered the position right then. I decided to accept, but asked for time to get my business in order. I agreed to be back in Tallahassee the first of June to begin my ministerial duties.

Ione and I dealt with the change. She planned to spend time with me in Florida working on her writing, counseling, and doing some workshops on her own. She would spend time at the Center in Idaho as well. She had some writing ideas and wanted to get serious about publishing. Earlier, we had produced many tapes for our tours and had spent a month at the Oregon coast writing our book, A Spiritual Tool Kit. After we had our motor home, we spent several days at a quiet lakeside park in Washington State, each writing on separate projects. This book was given birth there, and I knew that I would finish it "someday."

Right from the start, the experience in Tallahassee was a beautiful and positive one. The church grew dramatically; we paid off the mortgage and built an addition. The people and I experienced a love-in, a natural understanding of each other. I shared from the heart, and they loved it.

More healing took place deep within me. I was able to further release the Coeur d'Alene experience, see the lessons, have more mercy on myself and everyone involved. I saw that everyone was just doing what they felt was right at the time.

Tallahassee is 700 miles straight east of Houston, and Colleen and I were delighted we would be able see each other more often. The first Christmas, Colleen and David came to Tallahassee for a few days, then they drove on to Daytona Beach where his parents lived. Subsequently, I spent some of my vacation time in Houston. I was delighted when Colleen and David decided they were ready to become parents. On faith, I began a teddy bear needle point for a child's room during a Thanksgiving visit in Houston. Ione and I were there along with David's parents, Charles and Nellie. I blessed this stable and loving family network. I was happy for Colleen because she and David were so happy with each other. I liked him very much and appreciated that he was so solid and intelligent and not a substance abuser.

So often, daughters of alcoholics marry alcoholics. I was thankful that Colleen had broken that pattern, and other patterns of mine as well. She always had a good sense of self, a knowing that just having a man in her life would not be some kind of magic answer for her. I encouraged and coached her in this, but unless she'd had the inner resources for herself, the outcome would not have been so positive. Although Colleen had her own unique soul work to do, it was gratifying to observe that she didn't need to repeat my mistakes. I felt that I'd lived out the resolution of Florence's and Ruth's problems along with my own, so I rejoiced that my daughter was moving forward in a new way without repeating our old unskillful patterns.

By the end of January Colleen was pregnant, and I was ecstatic about the prospect of becoming a grandmother. She visited us in Tallahassee with her wondrous big tummy in June. We celebrated my birthday with Ione and Mary Beth, one of our new and special friends. Mary Beth is a pediatrician, which was of great interest to Colleen. We had a wonderful time together visiting some southern mansions in Thomasville, Georgia and eating lots of good food. At the church, I reveled in showing off my beautiful daughter. Everyone was cheering us on in our new roles as mother and grandmother. Besides that, Ione was set to be an "auntie," and we agreed to be as much like "Auntie Mame" as our energy would allow.

When Colleen went into labor, I jumped in the car and drove to Houston as fast as I could. It was September 19, 1990. Kelly Marie was less than a day old when I got to hold her, to marvel at her beauty, to rejoice with Colleen and David at the miracle of life they helped bring forth. Colleen and the baby came home after the second day, and I stayed on for ten days to help. This was a joyous time of togetherness and bonding. Colleen took an extended time away from her work so she could stay home with Kelly until after the first of the year.

Before Kelly's birth, Colleen had been comfortable with the idea of leaving the baby at a day care center. But it was different now. She was upset about the idea of leaving Kelly with strangers and hoped to find someone who would care for Kelly in their home, someone she could get to know and trust before leaving the baby. One afternoon, Colleen and I discussed this problem with Jean, my old and dear friend from high school.

We had always kept in touch, and I had never forgotten her kindness to Richard and me all those years ago when we came to Houston to try to begin a new life. After Colleen moved there, it had always been easy for me to see Jean every time I came to Houston because she and Colleen lived in the same area of the city. Although Jean and Colleen saw each other only when I was in town, they occasionally talked on the phone and felt like "family" to each other.

Jean had led a very stable life - lived in the same house for many years, raised four children and taken care of grandchildren. Currently, she was between projects. Colleen and I were dumbfounded but delighted when Jean declared, "Colleen, I can take care of the baby for you." We were so very thankful for this small miracle, for Jean's beautiful demonstration of loving kindness.

Three months later, I had the joyous experience of baptizing Kelly the Sunday before Christmas. We were in our new addition at church. We'd added space with a high ceiling and large windows which afforded a striking view of majestic pines. With new plants and a new entry area, along with Christmas decorations, everything looked beautiful. We were all proud of what had been accomplished at our church. I was also proud of my family. David's parents had come from Daytona Beach to be part of the service. Kelly, wonderfully well behaved sat happily on her father's lap. I felt waves of love and support from the people in the congregation, and I extended waves of love and support to them in return.

In ministerial school it was suggested that when a minister goes into a church, there needs to be a match between the energy of the people and the energy of the minister – its own kind of marriage. I understood the truth of this in Tallahassee. Why the chemistry worked so well, I didn't know for sure, but I was grateful that it did. Perhaps it was because Tallahassee was a college town and so many in the congregation were teachers. Tallahassee was also the state capital, home of the state agencies, so many social workers and other people in helping professions came to the church.

There was also a balance of young and old, singles and couples with children, male and female. The consciousness of the whole group was loving and open. In addition, the services were enhanced by the very beautiful and talented soloist and choir director Kathryn Hathaway.

I was truly blessed by the loving and professional board of directors who helped everything come together in an atmosphere of perfect harmony.

In addition, Ione and I made many new friends who continually found ways to do thoughtful things. On Ione's birthday friends invited us out for a celebration dinner and arranged to pick us up. We were ready and waiting, realizing they were running late. Then, a knock at the door. A young man in chauffeur's uniform told us, "Your chariot is waiting." Our friends were in the back of a white stretch limo, ready to begin the celebration. What a fun surprise!

However, in spite of the ideal circumstances, I began to realize a minister's job was nonetheless a very demanding and difficult one; I was exhausted much of the time. Consequently, I adjusted my schedule, obtained an answering machine, and monitored phone calls at home. Yet, there was always more that needed to be done. I knew better than to try to do it all myself, and there were many people who volunteered to help; yet, there was always more than I could comfortably handle. I felt the pressure to do more, mostly from myself. The church board was not pressuring me, and I had adequate time off. I was merely experiencing the demanding "real world" of ministry. I began to ask myself, "Is this how I want to spend the good years I have left?"

I was coming to realize that while I was in many ways suited to the ministry, in other ways I was not. I certainly loved the people, loved creating and giving talks and classes, loved "being there" for people in counseling. The problem came in doing it all at once, then handling the administrative and financial concerns besides. I was coming to realize that the gypsy life on the road and the time at the Holo Center in Idaho provided opportunity to love and to minister to people, while it also provided opportunity for rest and renewal. There was usually opportunity to take time off, whether hours, days, or weeks, when I felt the need.

In the midst of all these realizations about ministry, came the discovery that I was experiencing a new passage. Aging! I saw more wrinkles. I realized that although my spirit is ageless and eternal, I don't have forever in this particular earth suit. I wanted to spend more time with Kelly; I wanted to spend laid back time doing some writing; I wanted to do some more traveling; I wanted time for me; I wanted time to just be.

I began to think about bringing my time at the church to a close. However, I would not do this in haste. I wanted to leave with love and in an orderly fashion with the least trauma for the church. Therefore stayed a full year after I knew I would leave. I'd made many quick decisions in the past. I wanted this one to be slow, deliberate, right. Meanwhile, Ione and I made some plans for the future about writing projects, travel and workshops, further development of the retreat center in Idaho.

When I finally announced I would be leaving, people were sad, but at the same time understanding. What else could I have expected? At the going away party, the choir sang love songs to me, several individuals talked about specific things they appreciated, and I was given some lovely gifts. Many said they had especially benefitted from hearing about the healing experiences of little Julie May, my inner child. I tried to make it clear to these dear people how very much I would miss them.

They understood I would also need to leave Uni-kitty, an endearing stray yellow cat I fell in love with, befriended and fed who made the Unity grounds home. This cat loved people and greeted them before every event at the church. Everyone took an interest in petting and nourishing this cat, which was never given a name other than Uni-kitty. However, now that I was leaving, the people decided the cat's new name would be Julie May. Purr-fect! (Note: I later came to realize that I could have requested an assistant and more help. It did not occur to me or the board at the time.)

Summer 1991 Back in Idaho, the lazy summer is delicious. Many days are spent writing, reading, relaxing, quietly enjoying. It's not surprising that as I have all this time to honestly look deeper within myself, areas that still need attention and healing surface. I am definitely dealing with aging. I am almost sixty, a number that has no relationship to me! I affirm that I am an ageless, deathless, eternal Being. Yet, in this body, in this particular earth suit, there are limitations. This body will be released. The group of sub-personalities gathered together in the personality of Julie Keene will be dissolved. I, the Self, the essence of my Being will go on, but the particular life and circumstances of Julie Ireland Keene will be finished. I'm aware that this is a crucial passage, a pivotal point in my life. I have very important choices to make - not career choices, not relationship choices, not the kind of choices that seemed more crucial earlier in life. The important choice I must make now at this crossroads, at this passage point, is the choice of how I will age. Age I must - HOW I age is my choice.

Out of one model comes the option of decline into narrower mind set, regression into petulant childishness, self-pity, preoccupation with real and imaginary body ailments. A part of me could wail about the indignity of getting older, complain about lack of respect. Out of another model comes the option of responsible and welcomed Elderhood with an agenda to grow in wisdom, to continue to work with the patterns of learning that my soul has chosen, to continue to expand consciousness, not shrink it. I truly desire to live out this more expanded experience. I bless the opportunity to withdraw from the pressures of making money so that my mind and energy might move into pure playful creative endeavors. I am choosing to share my life experience and what I've learned from it with those who welcome that sharing. I am choosing to be open to whatever Spirit brings next. Because I believe that I am ongoing, ageless, eternal Spirit working through Earth School Lessons that continue on through life after life, I can know that what I learn and accomplish this lifetime is not wasted, not down the tubes when I die. I can know that if I allow myself to go unconscious, to narrow my vision, I only delay my own progress.

Much of my learning this time around has centered on recognizing my own worth. If I'd always known my worth, I would not have found it necessary to put so much energy into the attempt to prove it to myself and others. The release of this relentless pursuit has been gradual and painful, but each measure of progress has wonderful rewards. More creative expansive energy becomes available, and I revel in it! I'm excited about what will happen next in the great adventure of life.

Nonetheless, it's impossible to tie life up in a pretty bow and claim no more lessons or challenges; I now know that we all constantly choose how we will experience life. For many years, I was the victimized star of a melodramatic soap opera. Eventually, I learned to take responsibility for the role I was playing and realized that I was writer, director and producer as well. Gradually, the world of victims and villains was left behind, and I entered a more harmonious dimension.

In contrast to the soap opera, this dimension seems like a symphony. Of course there are still lessons to be learned and problems to be solved. The symphony encompasses minor chords as well as major ones . I must take the responsibility for this imperfect and unfinished symphony because I continually create it. When I depend on the human ego to guide me, the discordant result serves as my reminder to return to higher instruction and guidance, to love and the cosmic viewpoint. When I remember to tune into Divine Inspiration and Divine Love, the symphony reaches rapturous heights. I'm learning to bless each moment of the unfinished symphony of my life, its unpredictability, its mystery, even its continuing lessons.

CHAPTER TWELVE
MORE OF THE NEVER ENDING
ADVENTURE

"Life is a game. There is nothing
more exciting than to say 'yes' to
such a wild thing. I don't have anything
to lose. I can afford to be a fool."
-Byron Katie

In 1998, at the age of 66, I chose to leave the sheltered safe haven of
the Holo Center in North Idaho. I felt a strong pull to go back into
the pulpit ministry. My years at the Center with Ione and Masil were
life changing. Words can't express my gratitude to them for the love
and nurturing they shared with me over the years, let alone the traveling, the fun and adventures. But, I eventually came to the place where
I wanted to jump out of the nest. Although I was 66 at the time and
should have been content to rest in my rocking chair, something propelled me. Somehow I knew that I was not done yet. I am realizing
now that my gypsy foot and adventurous spirit will probably be with
me until the end.

When a minister has been out of the loop for more than a year and
wants back into the running, she must endure a process called rein-
statement. This involves a trip to Unity Village and an interview with
the ministers on a committee which decides your fate. I had been in
this situation before, so I was fairly calm and felt it would all be fine.

Around the table, looking at my varied career, the question was asked: "Given all the ups and downs and trials of ministry, why do you want back in?" The question surprised me and I went blank. Then before I could think of some kind of impressive answer, an answer just popped out of my mouth: "I don't know; I guess I must be crazy!" The ministers laughed along with me and I think that is what opened the door for me to continue on with my adventures in ministry.

As I began making preparations to find a new ministry, my birth mother Ruth made her transition into spirit. She died of a stroke and complications at age 80. My brother Ben called and asked me if I would come to the funeral in Michigan. His dad Ben would send the airfare. He also wanted to know if it was alright with me that I be listed in the obituary as her daughter. "Of course," I said. All through the years Ruth's husband Ben had kept the secret of Ruth's giving birth to me at a young age from his large Catholic family. He felt they were not all that happy that he married a divorced woman with two boys, let alone that she had been an unwed mother at 15.

Through the years, Ruth wanted to acknowledge me to everyone, but honored Ben's need to keep the secret. So why did he share it openly after she died? I believe it was because he felt it was something she wanted and he was going to make amends now and endure whatever consequences might follow. Ironically, the family welcomed me with open arms. "You look so much like your mother!" "You are beautiful." Ruth' s sister, my aunt Beulah, attended as well, and I certainly felt many loose ends were tied up.

Ten years later. Ben Sr. is plagued with several ailments: Diabetes, kidney failure, high blood pressure. Eventually he went on dialysis. My brother Ben had transferred back to Michigan so he could better look after his father, who insisted on living alone in the same house where he and Ruth had raised their family. Ben's condition continued to worsen to the point that Ben insisted his father come and live with him near Grand Rapids. Ben and his partner Rod learned to do the dialysis at home and were hoping for a few good years for Ben. However, it turned out to be only a few good months. I am grateful that I got to enjoy some of the good times with him the summer before his death. Ben's lake home has become a rendezvous for family and friends. That summer Colleen, brother Will and wife Margaret were all together with us to celebrate the 4th of July. We enjoyed going out on the pontoon boat and watching fireworks and taking lots of pictures. It was a happy time.

Somehow during Ben's many visits to the hospital, he contracted MERSA, the deadly virus that kills many, especially those as vulnerable as Ben. He died in September 2008, just 10 years after Ruth. This time, Ben asked me to officiate at his father's funeral service in Detroit, and I did. I reconnected with Ben's family and friends. Ruth's son Ron had previously passed on. Son Jack was there with his current wife. Ben and the family had the love and grace to continue their relationship with Jack's ex-wives, who were always part of family functions and who were at the funeral as well. Everyone seems to get along just fine. Just the way it should be.

Back to 1998. After Ruth's funeral I decided to ease back into ministry by taking an associate position under the minister in Salt Lake City. He was an easy going guy who had been in the class behind me in ministerial school. Actually, the board president recruited me to come down and lend a hand. I was up for an adventure that I thought would be a safe one to transition back into ministry. An adventure it would be. A learning and growing experience it would be. But in retrospect, I pronounce it all good. Starting out in Salt Lake as an associate to a minister who was mentally ill and paranoid, who was afraid I was trying to take over his ministry, my stay there was only five months. This is an example of a defense mechanism I have recently discovered about myself, although it's probably apparent to those who know me. I see what I want to see and hear what I want to hear. As a result I too often have needed to get myself out of situations I entered into in haste. Turns out that it is never too late to learn and grow!

Between that and the next ministry, in the fall of 1998, I went on a Unity trip to Switzerland, organized by my good friend Helice, co-minister with Richard Billings in Oak Park, Illinois. My daughter's dream was to go to Switzerland, so I invited her to come along. Her husband Dave stayed home with Kelly, and she says the trip was a high-light in her life. Of course such a mother-daughter trip was a wonderful highlight for me as well.

During this Switzerland trip, my dear mother Mary passed on. By then she was in her 90s and was in a nursing home. I had seen her regularly during the many visits to Michigan and had kept in close touch by phone. I could tell that physically and mentally she was nearing the end. Brother Will decided not to interrupt my trip. I didn't find out about her death until we returned home. I was not upset because I know there was nothing I could have done at that point. I had finished business with my wonderful mother several times over the years when we didn't know if she would make it or not. I love and bless her and miss her to this day. She has a very special place in my heart and I am eternally grateful for her loving care when I so desperately needed it.

Back from the trip, I put my things in storage in Salt Lake and began hunting for a new church. I tried out several places in Florida, was invited to Minneapolis area to try out. It was a beautiful church, but I didn't think I could endure the cold weather. Driving south, I stopped in St. George, Utah to guest speak. I didn't think of it as a "tryout," because I was focused on Florida. Yet, the city is in beautiful red rock high desert country, right on the southern border of Utah and 110 miles north of Las Vegas.

A friend in Salt Lake actually begged me to drive through Zion National Park, and as long as I was going through the area anyway, I did just that. I could not believe the beauty and grandeur of the place! I actually had to pull off the side of the road and weep because I was so moved. So, when I did not receive an invitation from a Florida church, I considered going back to St. George. The Unity group was a small study group when I spoke to them. At the time they begged me to come back and to grow them into a church. Since I had fallen in love with the geography anyway, I decided to come back out west. It took about a year to get the group acknowledged as a church.

Meanwhile, I met a widower who was part of the church there and after a short courtship, we were married at the church. Helice came down from Oak Park and officiated at the ceremony, and friends came from Salt Lake; Carol Hale Armor came from the church in Tallahasse,Florida to be my matron of honor. Brothers Ben and Will came and walked me down the aisle. A Beautiful "happily ever after" scenario! Not quite. I had another lesson to learn. When it comes to men in my life, I tend to jump in without allowing enough time to know them at depth. Going out and having fun is one aspect, but day to day living is when truth reveals itself. And of course I saw what I wanted to see and not the warning signals.

I could say I regret this marriage that lasted only fourteen months, but in spite of the drama and trauma involved, I do bless the experience. I discovered that there was a lot more to learn about human nature, including my own. It has been an exercise in forgiveness and realizing there is nothing to forgive. I came to understand the consequences and the suffering of an unhealed person and the unwillingness to do anything about it. I can only have compassion for Howard and have always wished him well. When I realized that the verbal abuse was wearing me down and that I could not remain in such a hostile environment, I knew I had to just walk away. We went to a counselor once. Howard's

185

true nature came out loud and clear when he said he was a very good supervisor on his job and he knew he was right. The male counselor said, "that may works fine on the job, but it can't work in a marriage." That was the end of counseling as far as Howard was concerned.

I loved the geography and the town of St. George, Utah. In this beautiful red rock country, high desert, people play golf all winter. And I loved that it was only fifty miles from Zion National Park. I lost count of how many times I went there. I would have liked to stay in that area, but I could not grow the church enough in that Mormon territory to sustain a full salary, which I needed at the time. It was in St. George Utah that Brigham Young built his first tabernacle. So, out went the resumes again. This time to Gainesville, Florida.

I love the town of Gainesville, Florida. Home of the University of Florida Gators! It is a fairly small town with a lot of big town amenities. Here, I made wonderful friends and really loved the little church. I was fortunate enough to rent a condo right on a lake with a lovely heated pool not far from my door. I reconnected with a dear friend from Tallahassee who had a lake home nearby, and spent a lot of time with her.

So, what were the lessons? Two major ones. To begin, the church had been without a minister for two years. Two women who were working on becoming licensed teachers were running the church. I liked them and was sure that we could all work together. Was this more seeing what I wanted to see? Pat was the church administrator; Terry was on the board and did all kinds of things with and for the church. The by-laws had been changed to give the administrator equal authority with the minister. I did not even take note of that at first.

Before long, it became apparent that I was to be the minister in name only and the ladies would run the church. Of course they had friends on the board. I didn't stand a chance. I was ready to cut and run. But then I decided to stand up. I called Unity and a senior minister in the area. We called a congregational meeting to change the by-law back to what Unity recommends. By a vast majority the congregation supported me. Pat and Terry left, took their friends with them and started their own group. I wished them well. That's what they needed all along - their own group.

All went extremely well for another four years. But in ministry, one never knows when an explosion can come from out of the blue. I had been going up to Michigan for vacation every summer to be with brother Ben at his lake home near Grand Rapids. At the end of July 2005, when I got back home from vacation, a bombshell awaited me.

First, the back story: During a church workshop with Paul Ferrini, a Course in Miracles teacher, I met Ed. I could tell that he was in some kind of pain, and he asked if he could speak with me in private. He confessed that he was on parole - had served time as a sex offender. He is a Viet Nam vet who suffered bouts of depression. At a time when his fiancee was away visiting her family, he was lonely. He got on the internet and solicited sex from what turned out to be a minor. Then, the minor turned out to be an undercover cop and he was arrested and spent time in prison. Luckily he was caught before he could even think about actually carrying out a plan. This was a first offense. Currently he was living with his fiancee who stood by him. (I performed a wedding ceremony for them later.)

The question from him: "Is it ok if Gayle and I come to church?" I didn't even have to think about the answer. "Of course, " I replied, "but, you won't be able to be involved in any way with the youth - and you know that I'm going to keep an eye on you." So, Ed and Gayle came to church for several months with no incident or problem. I believe this couple was receiving much healing and guidance as they were determined to get past these circumstances .

When I got back from Michigan I received a phone call from Donna. Donna was a person whom I had mentored, put on the platform, supported in every way. "Do you know we have a pervert coming to church?' she asked. While I was in Michigan the local newspaper had "outed" the sex offenders, by publishing their names and addresses in a special section of the paper. "Are you talking about Ed? I asked. "Yes," she responded, " and you have to tell him he can't come to church." I said I could not do that because he had been there for months with no problem. At that point Donna became hysterical and said she was going to call all the mothers and others in the church and have me fired if I did not comply with her request. Here we go again!

The church split into two camps, most of the people lined up behind me, but a loud handful of people would not stop. Meetings were held. The previous minister who had retired but still came to church, stood by me and tried to reason with these people, but they shouted him down. Donna threatened to sue the church and I can't even remember all the threats. The board was supportive of me, but allowed the people to continue their agenda of disruption.

A way out for me came in the form of an offer from an affluent congregant for three months salary if I wanted to leave. I decided to accept this offer and look elsewhere. It was very difficult to leave the dear friends I had made, but I felt in the long run it would be best. So, out went the resumes one more time. Looking over the list of openings, I saw that Garden Park Unity in Cincinnati was open. I talked to Ben about it because he had once been in stationed in Ohio.

Ben has recently retired from the postal inspection service, which is considered federal law enforcement. He said Cincinnati was a very nice city with lots to do. Also, Ione and I had been at Garden Park Unity several years before. My friend from Unity ministerial school, Sylvia Scherer lived there and we had parked our motor home at her farm at that time. I remembered the beautiful church grounds and the fabulous huge stained glass window of Jesus walking on the water. It felt good to throw my hat in this ring. I considered some other places too, but after I visited - tried out - at the church, it felt like the right and perfect place for me. And so it has proved to be. No major problems, no uproar, - lots of love and goodwill.

About this time my son Robert read a newspaper article about new brain surgery being performed at the University hospital in Ann Arbor, Michigan. The surgery's purpose is to help those people whose seizures cannot be controlled with medication. Although Robert had been on seizure medication since early childhood, his seizures were never completely controlled. He never knew when he would have a minor or major seizure. Because he had more than one type of seizure, getting them under control was a major challenge. He suffered for years never being able to drive or hold down a job.

He became an excellent house husband, but he was never really happy or satisfied with his life. There was a phone number to call at the end of the article about the surgery and Robert called and made an appointment. Grayling is about 200 miles north of Ann Arbor. Robert's wife Lee Ann, drove him down there for several appointments to determine whether or not the surgery would be of benefit to him. Finally, the doctors decided that he was a good candidate. I can't begin to describe the exact procedure, but it consisted of going into part of his brain. He was released from the hospital in just a few days with instructions to keep taking his medication.

As the days and weeks went by without any seizures, Robert's attitude and outlook on life mellowed considerably. His goal was to go six months seizure free so that he could get his driver's license. Five months after the surgery, he had a minor seizure, but he was able to deal with it. "The doctor said my medication might need to be adjusted and not to worry if I had a seizure."So, he patiently counted the days and weeks until he could go apply for his driver's license. Five months later I got a phone call from Robert. He was in the depths of despair because he had yet another seizure. I was truly concerned about his well being; he seemed to have lost all hope of things ever being different.

Over the years, I had talked to Robert about the spiritual element of life. After I started TM myself, I had him take the course. He was initiated and given a mantra, but I don't think he used it for any length of time. He was definitely closed to the ideas I knew would help. Finally, I gave it up and just started holding him in the light of prayer. It seemed in this dark hour that there was no avenue of relief. Earlier I had written out a message to Robert and Lee and put it in my Bible, which gave me comfort (but I did not send it to them because I felt they would not be open to such a message.) I'll share it here:

Robert and Lee Ann,

I think of you with love. I pray for you with faith. I think of you with confidence. I believe in you. I pray for you with assurance. I believe in the God in you. I think of you in terms of understanding. I may not see why your life takes the direction it does, but I have the understanding to realize that you must follow your own inner direction. Because I know that God is with you, I am willing to release you to God's care. I am willing to forego criticism or judgment and see you as God sees you - a growing, unfolding spiritual being. As I think of you, I think of the good that is in you. I praise and appreciate your good qualities. I see them magnified and increased. As I pray for you, I place you in God's care. I release all anxiety concerning you. I am at peace concerning you. I am thankful because I know that God in with you, your help, your strength, your sure and certain guide. Amen.

A few days after Robert's despairing phone call, I heard from him again. He told me about walking around his neighborhood totally dejected, and finding himself in front of the parish priest's house. He never went to church and did not know the priest, but in his desperation, he knocked on the door. When the priest answered, Robert asked, "Will you pray for me?" He was invited into the house; the priest prayed with him and also put healing oil on his head. That day Robert was given the gift of caring and hope. Of course, I was delighted and felt that my prayers were being answered.

Robert started going to the church and even took classes in preparation to join. He and the priest became friends. Then the priest was transferred and the people running the class decided Robert had not done well enough in the class and therefore was not eligible to become a church member. It was a miracle in itself that Robert took all this in stride. He stopped going to church, but he said: "I can pray at home." I do believe he felt a connection to Spirit. It didn't matter from what tradition it came from.

This time, six months went by without a seizure. Robert studied to pass the written exam and did well; then he passed the driving test and received his license. What a joy it was for him. In all the months since the surgery he was changing. Lee Ann said it was like being married to a new person - and she meant that in the most positive sense. I felt like I finally had my son back.

Over the years, Robert would go through periods of being very angry with me because he blamed me for his misery. He never sent a Mother's Day or birthday card, although I never stopped sending him cards and giving him support. I learned what unconditional love was, and I came to see him as my teacher in many ways. But now, I began to receive birthday and Mother's Day cards and even some very sweet gifts! A plaque for the wall came for Mother's Day with the words: "Life began with waking up and loving my Mother's face." Of course, my heart melted and I cried tears of joy and release.

Robert began looking for jobs and actually had some business cards made up advertising his availability for yard work and odd jobs. And he has been quite successful at this. The relief from his seizures has given him a new attitude and a new life, and I am so happy for him and so grateful for this miracle. A few years have gone by now and although he has had some minor setbacks, he is on track and doing very well. I am reminded of the words of Eleanor Roosevelt: "You must never, for whatever reason, turn your back on life." I can only say amen to that.

Another miracle was about to unfold. I had long ago forgiven and re-leased Duane. I came to understand my part in our soap opera, and I only wished him well. He remained with Phyllis over the years of ups and downs, and I wished them both well. I occasionally received news of them from Colleen and Robert. After his surgery Robert sometimes drove his pickup truck the 50 miles south to see his dad, and Colleen saw her dad whenever she came up to Michigan.

Then in July 2007while I was visiting my brother Ben at his lake home near Grand Rapids, Colleen gave me her dad's cell phone number and said I should call him. I knew that he had cancer surgery earlier. He seemed to be doing well and had gone back to work. At the time I called him, he was working away from home at a job in Detroit. He never worked at anything else besides pipe line work, and most of the years he was a superintendent.

Sitting on the deck of Ben's home overlooking the lake while we talked, Duane and I had a very moving and satisfying conversation. What he wanted to tell me was: "I'm so sorry for the way I treated you." Of course, my heart melted and I assured him that I had long ago forgiven and wished him the best. Then, we talked about his cancer. He had been in great pain for quite awhile before he was finally diagnosed properly and one of his kidneys was removed. By then, the cancer had traveled to his lungs. He was on chemo for awhile, but it make him so sick that he decided to stop it and just go ahead and live for as long as he could.

He said: "I don't know how long I have, but I know I will see Richard." And we talked about his grandparents and parents and my Mama Mary and other people whom we both knew who were now gone. We agreed that he would be able to reunite with them when his time to die might come. We talked for about a half hour, which turned out to be a moving and heartfelt conversation. I am so grateful for that conversation.

A year later, the next July, I was once again vacationing at Ben's home and Colleen had come up from Texas for her vacation. Less than two weeks earlier, Duane had his bladder removed. He agreed to meet us in Clare, near his home. Robert and Lee came down from Graying, Colleen and I drove up from Grand Rapids, and Duane's daughter Jill who lived next door to Phyllis and Duane drove him. We were grouped at a round table in the Doherty Hotel dining room. Phyllis did not come because her mental condition was deterioriating and she did not want to go into public places.

It was obvious that Duane was in pain, so we didn't linger over dinner. We went outside and took several photos of Colleen and her dad, Robert and Lee and Dad. Then more photos of Duane, me, Colleen and Robert, and Colleen with her sister Jill - even one of Duane and me. After that, Jill suggested that we follow her and Duane back out to the farm where they lived. Duane said his good-byes and needed to go back to his bedroom and rest. During the process, we hugged and I said to him: "I have always loved you." He managed to say, "me too."

We went in the house to say hello to Phyllis. I didn't know what to expect. I had not seen her in years. She hugged me like a long lost friend, and it seemed totally natural, which I took as a sign that we had indeed left the past issues and irritations behind. We did not linger. Colleen went back to the bedroom to and tell her dad goodbye and we left.

Duane just went downhill from there, ending up in Hospice. His daughters who live in the area kept Colleen informed and Colleen shared that with me. He died on October 6, 2008. Colleen asked me to go to the funeral with her and Kelly. "I can't do it without you," she said. Of course, I agreed. So Colleen and Kelly flew into Cincinnati and then the three of us drove up to Michigan for the funeral.

This turned out to be quite a long and drawn out process. He died on Monday and was not buried until the next Saturday because Phyllis wanted to be sure all his pipe line people could get there. She thought Saturday would be easier for them. So, we drove up on Wednesday and stayed at the Day's Inn in Clare for three nights. We left right after the funeral because I needed to get back to Cincinnati for Sunday services.

Oh, the memories. Duane was in the very same funeral home from which Richard had been laid out, and then buried right next to Richard in the cemetery near Mt. Pleasant. Of course, I saw many people who remembered me from years ago when Duane and I were married. However, I made a successful effort to stay in the background. After all, Phyllis was the widow.

Duane and I had lived in Rosebush, half way between Clare and Mt. Pleasant when we were married. Richard went to school there and his best friend was a boy named Larry Galgoci who lived just down the street from us. Driving back from a visit with Jill, Colleen and I passed through Rosebush and I saw a sign that said Galgoci's Repair Shop. I decided to stop in and was told that Larry was eating lunch in the restaurant down the road with his guy friends. I felt compelled to stop by the restaurant. I walked in, saw the table of men and said I was looking for Larry. He recognized me and excused himself so we could talk.

He had heard about Duane's passing. We talked about Richard and what a good time they had together growing up until Richard died. Of course Larry is married and has children and grand children. Having a warm conversation with him felt so good - almost like "what life might have been for Richard." We parted with a hug and well wishes.

At the funeral home, a close friend who had been with Duane near the end and who would be participating in the eulogy at the funeral service, took me aside. He said that he had something to share with me, a message from Duane. He said that Duane had been very clear and insistent that he relay the message. "Tell her I love her." It was a most unexpected message from beyond and one that I appreciated from the bottom of my heart. I do want to make it clear that this in no way had anything to do with his relationship with Phyllis. Just because he sent love to me didn't mean that he didn't love Phyllis. After all, they had been together for 47 years!

Finally, came the day of the funeral in the same Methodist church where Richard's funeral service took place. The only difference was that the building itself was new and expanded and in a location a few blocks away. I was sitting in the back in an aisle seat, determined to hold it together and to "stay out of the way." Robert, Colleen, Duane and Phyllis' girls and families were in a side room saying their final good-byes before the casket was closed.

Then, out they came in procession. Phyllis was walking with Robert on one side and a son-in-law on the other. She looked up, saw me and said, "Come and sit with us; you're part of the family." And so I joined in with the rest of the procession and went up front. I sat between Robert and Duane's sisters. As I sat down, my heart absolutely bust open from Phyllis' act of kindness. I sobbed gut wrenching sobs, but silently. I was shaken to the core. Afterwards, I wiped my tears and held hands with those on each side and moved as in a dream through the rest of the day.

That open hearted soft expansive feeling has never totally left me and I doubt if it ever will. With that one gesture, all less than loving words or interactions were wiped out and only love remains - love between me and Phyllis and between Duane and me and including everyone in a huge circle. I can see that all the boundaries and possessiveness are as nothing. We are all just souls who only did the best we knew at any given time. We are all learning and growing. In the end, we are all one.

In August I decided to give Phyllis a call to see how she was doing. A family friend answered the telephone and informed me that daughter Karen and her husband had taken Phyllis to an extended care facility in Clare because they could no longer care for her properly. After the funeral, several incidents had occurred that made it clear that she needed to be tended to full time and it would be too much for Karen and Greg.

No doubt I will stop and visit Phyllis when I am in Michigan. How can I feel anything but love for her now? I have now retired (at least temporarily) from church ministry and will be spending some time in the summers in Michigan with Ben and his partner Rod at the lake house. I will be living with Colleen and Kelly in Texas part of the year and traveling and visiting in Michigan the remainder of the time. My family - (Ben and Rod, Will and Margaret, Robert and Lee Ann, Colleen and Kelly) are all so aware that our soul's sojourn here is brief and when we get nearer to the end of it, we tend to treat it with more respect. We treasure our time together because we realize on a deeper level that we don't have forever. Although, in truth, we do have forever in Spirit, and we will be with our loved ones forever because love IS forever.

As I write this, my last Sunday at Garden Park has come and gone. I have decided to retire – for now. I am grateful to Garden Park Unity for making these last few years in pulpit ministry so rewarding and drama and trauma free. I can compare it to Tallahassee, which was also such a supportive place with no uproar. I know I will keep many of the friends I have made here and I hope to come back once in awhile to visit friends and to guest speak and maybe present a workshop.

I will also continue with an internet ministry I started several months ago. Along with that, I will travel, guest speak and do some workshops when I am invited to do so. I can't quite lay it all down. But at 77, I feel the need for more time and space for myself. I love to write - maybe I'll actually finish that novel I started while I was in Idaho! I want to wander around the country, exercise my gypsy foot, visit my friends and other churches and just be. . I have my wonderful companion of six years, an 11 pound Shih Tsu named Bella. She has been a wonderful church dog - does not bark, jump, loves everybody, and can sit in the middle of a class or workshop and sleep and exude love. And another bonus: she loves to ride in the car and has always been great on long trips, such as we used to take between Florida and Michigan. What a gift!

The lyrics of the following song summarize how I'm feeling right now. Ione and I used to sing this as we rolled around the country in our motor home:

> No matter where I wander
> No matter where I roam
> I play my part with a happy heart
> The whole wide world's my home.
> The future lies before me,
> Like an offer, now a vow.
> The past is dead like a book I've read,

I'm living here and now.
–The Oneness Space

February 2010

MORE UPDATES: When it comes down to it, life is a series of updates! Life goes on and lifetimes end. Change is constant. I have been in Sugar Land, Texas with my daughter since the first of November 2009. In early December, my dear brother Will dropped over in a shopping mall in Michigan while Christmas shopping with his wife Margaret. He never regained consciousness and passed on a few days later. He had told Margaret that he wanted me to officiate at his memorial service, which I consider a great honor. Will was not a church person and only came to a church when I was speaking a time or two. He loved me and didn't want to offend me, so he asked if I would be upset if he didn't come. My answer was, "Of course not." Will was a wonderful mentor and loving supportive brother over the years, - always kind and always laid back. Will's other requests were that he be immediately cremated, no viewing etc. and that the memorial be held in the meeting room of his favorite restaurant on the St. Claire River. Margaret arranged everything as he requested. During the service several large tankers floated by and we watched out the big windows. Earlier Will and a friend shared a sailboat and spent lots of happy times in the area.

Most people, including myself, have to work pretty hard to get to the place where we are centered, where nothing out there upsets us, where we just live in an emotional space of equilibrium. All this just came naturally to Will. I never saw him really upset. The most challenge I saw him go through was when he was recovering from esophageal cancer and could not eat solid food for months, and so he was uncomfortable and weak physically. At that time he gave in to his family's urging and took something for depression. Thankfully, he fully recovered and had several good years back to his "normal" easygoing self before he made his final exit at age 80.

I remember back when it was a big deal to do a workshop exercise such as:

"What would you do if you knew you had only six months to live?" Such a question had a degree of unreality for me although I dutifully came up with answers that were helpful. Now I do a similar exercise often within myself: "If I drop over tomorrow or in five minutes, have I finished my business? Have I done what is important for me to do? I can answer Yes to that question. However, that does not mean that I have stopped working on myself, pushing myself to grow psychologically and spiritually. My aim is to do that until I take the last breath.

Right now, I am reading the second volume of a set of five. Each volume is about 800 pages of fine print - and packed with incredible information and inspiration. When in ministerial school one of our teachers, Ed Rabel, was a fan of "The Work" (sometimes called the 4th Way) and encouraged us to buy this set of books. I didn't have the time or inclination to get into them until last fall, but I'm now loving them: Psychological Commentaries on the Teaching of Gurdjieff & Ouspensky. They are a treasure trove and out of print except for volume five. I feel so fortunate to have the whole set and that I finally am benefitting from them after all these years of moving around. I got rid of a lot of things, but always hung onto them, never even realizing how important they would turn out to be for me.

As I look back on all the soap opera events in my life, I am quite disconnected from them and have been for quite some time. The more healing I've done, the more I have taken the lessons and the gifts and left the useless unnecessary suffering behind. I am blessed and grateful for the teachers and the teachings and the opportunities I've had this lifetime.

I plan to travel and do workshops and speaking engagements while visiting friends, and I plan to do all this at a balanced pace. But one never knows what tomorrow will bring, so the only sane approach is to take it one day at a time. My goal is to bless and to enjoy each day, to express my love and creativity as much as I possibly can and to just surrender to the process of living in Spirit.

I have always admired Grandma Moses who began seriously painting in her sixties. She got better and better as the years went by and did some of her best work at 99 and 100. She died at 101 in a nursing home, but only after the doctors took away her paints because they wanted her to rest more. So, as long as I'm able I'll be up to something - and we'll know what it is as it comes along!

My latest internet message:
"It's never too late to raise a little hell."
-Granny D at age 94

I was in the car and listening to public radio when I heard about the passing of Granny D just a few days ago. She was a hundred years old and going strong up to the end. At the age of 89 she began her 3,200 mile walk across country from Los Angeles to Washington D.C. This was to highlight the need for campaign reform that would remove unregulated "soft" money from political campaigns. Granny - Doris Haddock - traveled as a pilgrim, walking until given shelter, fasting until given food. Because of the generosity of strangers she met along the way, Doris never went without a meal or a bed. She trekked through over 1,000 miles of desert, climbed the Appalachia Range in blizzard conditions and even skied 100 miles after a historic snowfall made roadside walking impossible. When she arrived in Washington D.C., several dozen members of Congress walked the final miles with her.

Wow! It's amazing how the universe works! I have been going through a soul searching period lately. I have discovered that I cannot pull the plug and just sit back and really retire. I have rested up, and caught up with myself, and that is a good thing. I do this internet ministry and that is a very good thing for me. I hope and pray it's a good thing for you too. But there is always more. I'm about to head out to Florida for six weeks - then back here - and who know what?

Changes are afoot! Exactly where that all leads to, I don't know right now. All I know is that I'm not done yet! Certainly finding out about Granny D has served to underline my intention. I have been reading and re-reading Lesson 194 in Course in Miracles: <u>I place my future in the hands of God.</u> The more deeply and fully I can do this, the more peace and optimism about the future I feel. And so it can be with you too.

What is the spiritual lesson in all this? Probably several, but the one that comes to mind to point out here is this: "Thoughts held in mind produce after their kind." "Change your thinking, change your life." It all starts with our thinking and moves to the emotional center and then the moving center of us. We can feel new energy and enthusiasm for life, but we do have to be open and receptive to the truth and inspiration that comes to us from all around us. If we think we know it all and have it all together, we shut the door to further growth.

That's why I love to hear inspirational stories about people who keep the doors of their minds open up until the very end. We don't have to set out on a 3200 mile trek across country. But we do have to be flexible and willing to adjust and adapt to what's going on. My aim and intention in this lifetime is to grow psychologically and spiritually. So whatever it takes to accomplish that, I'm willing to do. I have a tremendous love for people and a desire to mix and mingle with them. Of course, I need my alone time as well, but that is the balance we all need.

I have been sequestered in a sense here living in my daughter's house and keeping busy preparing new workshop material and getting my ducks in a row so to speak. Now, it time to venture out again, and I have realized that I don't want to make excuses about what I can't do because I am aging. I'm still a spring chicken in spite of my chronological age - I've got lots of miles in me yet. I remind myself that it's never too late to raise a little "heaven."

I can see the importance for all of us in renewing ourselves each day. There is that in us that would keep us in a rut. So we carpet it and stay there for awhile. Most of us have done that. But if we're lucky, the time comes when we do feel Divine Discontent and we look for tools that will renew our quest for advancement and renew our zest for living. Charles Fillmore, founder of Unity, affirmed at 94 that he "fairly sizzled" with zest and enthusiasm for life. So, no matter what our age at this point, let's live it to the fullest. Let's keep the doors and windows of our soul open to the instruction and guidance of Holy Spirit. Let's truly embrace and enjoy the grand adventure of life!

God Bless You in Every Way. – and maybe I'll see you in my travels "on the road again!"

CHAPTER THIRTEEN
TRANSFORMING TOOLS AND
TECHNIQUES

"I am here to be truly helpful.
I am here to represent him who sent me.
I will be healed as I let Him teach me to heal."
Course in Miracles

The following techniques and exercises are both spiritual and psycho-logical. In truth these two aspects of our reality cannot be separated. Growth in one area automatically fosters progress in the other. These particular methods have been key factors in my own healing, growth, and evolution thus far. Please know that there is not one magic answer that will fix your life for once and for all; higher levels of awareness and love are always calling to us. Thus, these experiences are offered to you, not as the ultimate "big fix", but as helpful techniques. Certainly, in-teraction with a professional therapist can be of enormous value. These tools and techniques are not a substitute for that. It would be good to find a trusted person to work together with you so that you could aid one another in moving through these exercises and experiences.

REGULAR MEDITATION: A SOLID FOUNDATION

WHY MEDITATE? 1) SPIRITUAL GROWTH - Teachers through the ages have emphasized the importance of turning within to find Truth/God/The Ultimate Reality. If indeed our purpose here in Earth School is spiritual growth, and if meditation is vital to that growth, we want to take it seriously. 2) PRACTICAL BENEFITS - Meditators report more energy and harmony in daily life, greater understanding of others, more peace with themselves, and improved health.

WHAT IS MEDITATION? 1) A TECHNIQUE - Meditation calms the mind and rests the body, which provides mental and physical benefits. It can be helpful even without a spiritual or religious intention. Many physicians recommend that their patients meditate to lower blood pressure and stress. 2) AN ALTERED STATE OF CONSCIOUSNESS - Meditation changes the brain wave pattern (which can be measured by an EEG). It differs from the waking, sleeping, or hypnotic state. It is unique in that it produces rest and alertness at the same time. While meditating, you can open your eyes and stop meditating at will so that any interruption or emergency can be attended to. Meditation is not an "out of it" trance state. 3) LISTENING PRAYER - Many think of prayer as talking to God, reaching outward and upward. In meditation you relax into your own inner silence, a sacred place of connection between the human and the Divine.

GUIDELINES FOR BEGINNING MEDITATORS: 1) BE CONSISTENT - Meditate every day, if only for five minutes. Twenty to thirty minutes twice each day is very beneficial. At times, you may be seeking specific guidance. However, it's important to meditate every day, even if you don't feel the need for guidance. It's important to meditate every day whether you feel like it or not. 2) SET A REGULAR TIME EACH DAY - Set a regular time, or you often won't "get around to it." Choose times when interruptions are least likely, times best for you. It's better to meditate before a meal or when your stomach is not full so that the digestive process does not interfere with the meditation. 3) GUARD AGAINST INTERRUPTIONS - Try to choose a time when you're alone. If that's not possible, let your family know you are meditating, and ask them to cooperate. Mute the phone, and answering machine. People with small children find it easier to meditate early in the morning, during nap time, or after the children are in bed at night. 4) PROPER POSITION - is sitting with the spine erect, unless you are able to lie down and not fall asleep. Always keep your spine straight.

TWO SPECIFIC MEDITATION TECHNIQUES: The following methods should be very helpful, especially as you begin. As you become more experienced or do extended reading, you may find ways that work better for you. There is not only ONE way. However, it is wise, when learning, to stay with one method for a period of time. I learned a mantra meditation and used only that method for several years before moving into variations and expansions. Others use many methods from the beginning. Do what is comfortable for you; you can trust yourself.

BREATHING - Close your eyes and become aware of your breathing. Inhale deeply and slowly and count to yourself on each exhale. Inhale, exhale and count one. Inhale, exhale and count two. Inhale, exhale and count three. Inhale, exhale and count four. Begin again. Inhale, exhale and count one...Continue in this pattern, never exceeding four counts before beginning again. Keep gently and silently counting. Feel yourself relax into the center of LIGHT and LOVE, surrounded with LIGHT and LOVE, filled with LIGHT and LOVE.

MANTRA - Allow your mind to rest upon a word/sound. Choose one that feels right for you. Some examples: ONE - OM - GOD - JESUS. Other thoughts will naturally arise. When this happens, just gently go back to the mantra. The pace will vary. The mantra may stretch out or it may become shorter. There will be spaces where there is no mantra and no thoughts. Just gently move back to the mantra when you become aware that you have moved away from it. Don't make an effort to hang onto the mantra. Let it go as it will, then gently come back to it.

WHAT TO DO ABOUT THOUGHTS AND OUTSIDE NOISES:
Your mind will often wander. That's the nature of the mind. Some meditations will seem to be mostly random thoughts. This is true for me after thirty years of meditation practice. That's OK. Thoughts are a natural and normal part of meditation. Just keep bringing your mind back to the focus of the meditation. Gently release the thought when you become aware of it, when you realize that your mind has wandered. Move back to the focus - breathing, mantra, whatever. Although you want to try to meditate away from noise, you won't always be able to control your environment. Dogs bark. Pans rattle. People talk in the distance. Treat these noises and distractions exactly like you treat a random or stray thought. Notice it - be neutral about it - release attention from it. Easily and gently go back to the focus of the meditation.

Sometimes what seems to be a very important idea or insight may flash into your mind and will not easily be put aside. When this happens, write a word or two on a notepad. (Always meditate with a pad and pencil right beside you.) When the meditation is over, you can write about the idea in more detail. Take plenty of time to shift into your normal waking state, a minimum of three or four minutes, before you begin your regular activity. This transition time is important. It helps you carry the calm and centered state of meditation back out into your regular activity.

BE THE FACILITATOR OF YOUR OWN LIFE HEALING

There is absolutely no experience that the power of God, the power of Love, cannot transform and heal. In Spirit there is no time as we know it. Thus, it is possible for you to enlist the aid of Spirit as you confront and deal with your past pain. These past experiences CAN be transformed. You CAN be set free! You need only a sincere desire and the will to begin. I believe along with the English poet Tennyson that "God is nearer than breathing, closer than hands and feet." You may call upon this Presence and Power to join with you in present time, past time, future time. God is not limited by time or space. In the experiences that follow you will use the power of your active imagination. Some people are naturally good at visualization and can create vivid pictures in their minds at will. Others have difficulty "seeing" themselves in a place or situation, as most of these exercises suggest. However, you have your own unique way of using your imagination. One way is not better than another way. For example, instead of seeing a vivid picture, you might have a general impression about being under a tree or walking through a sunlit meadow, or you might just feel in a tactile way what it would be like to be there. When you read a descriptive passage in a book, you have your own way of relating to and experiencing that description. When you listen to a tape or hear a radio drama, you find a way to "be in" the action. Sometimes you might see pictures, have physical feelings and feel emotions all at once. Your experiences are different at different times. As you enter into the following exercises in your own way, be confident that you will experience the healing and the benefit that is exactly right for you.

THE FIRST STEPS IN EACH OF THE EXERCISES:

1) Find a time when you won't be interrupted or hurried for at least half an hour. No phone calls. Do just one exercise at a sitting. There is no particular right order. You will be drawn to the one that's right for you when you need it. There is great value in completing all the exercises, but in your own time. You might want to have writing materials or a tape recorder with you so that you can record and process your experience. You might want to record this first step because you will use it often.

2) Take several slow deep breaths. Think with each breath, "I breathe in PEACE. I breathe out ALL ELSE." Feel your body relaxing. Beginning at the very tip of your toes, see, feel, imagine a warm comfort-

ing golden light begin to slowly travel up your body. Relaxing, warming, soothing, energizing. Move the light through the feet and ankles, calves, knees, thighs, pelvic area. Slowly. Up through the solar plexus and chest, up the back, through the neck and up into the head, slowly flowing down the shoulders and arms to the tip of the fingers. The light is absorbed into all cells and organs of your body, revitalizing, soothing, relaxing. Now the light radiates out from your body and forms a cocoon of light with you in the center, so safe, so secure. Now, you become aware that you are not alone. A beautiful loving Being of Light is here to protect and guide, to extend unconditional love. (You may think of this Being as your Higher Power, your Christ Self, your Higher Self, or even Jesus the Christ.) You are ready to begin.

FIND AND NURTURE YOUR INNER CHILD

1) Relaxing exercise (described above) 2) Find yourself in a sunlit meadow. (Remember that your Light Being is with you.) Wild flowers abound. A path leads down to a gently flowing stream. As you walk along this path, you notice a big shade tree by the river. As you come closer to the inviting shade of the tree, you see that a child is under this tree waiting for you to approach. You begin to realize that this is YOUR OWN inner child. Notice his/her age, facial expression, attitude. 3) Be aware that this child has something to tell you or something to show you. Be open to receive this communication. If the child has anger or distrust toward you, ask what you need to do to change that. Tell the child that you will always be available to love and support him/her because now you have the aid of the Light Being. 4) When you feel you have finished your dialogue with the child, you and the child embrace - the Light Being embraces the child - then you, the child, and the Light Being embrace. You feel your heart expand, and then you, the child, and the Light Being merge into One beautiful essence. (Repeat often and notice the positive results in your life.)

ANOTHER HEALING EXPERIENCE FOR YOU AND YOUR CHILD BEGINNING FROM THE MOMENT OF CONCEPTION:

1. Relaxing exercise (described previously)
2. Imagine yourself as a tiny point of consciousness that has just arrived in your mother's womb. There is no time or space in Spirit. You and the Light Being now in this moment have the power to fill this womb with love and light, the power to dissolve any pain or trauma. Feeling safe now with the Light Being, you begin to focus upon the first month of life in the womb. Memories may or may not arise. If a painful memory comes up, allow the Light Being to fill this memory with Light and Infinite Love. Observe any changes this brings about. If a happy memory arises, enjoy it, bless it, and then move on. If no specific memory arises, fill this space and time with Light and Love, bless it and move on. Repeat this process for all the months before your physical birth. 3) **PHYSICAL BIRTH** - The Light Being has surrounded you in a protective shield that allows you to experience a smooth entrance into Earth School. Any pain or trauma, remembered or un-remembered, is now given to the Light Being to transmute into only of Love and Light. 4) **ENTER EARTH SCHOOL** - The first thing you see is the smiling, welcoming face of Love, the Being of Light. The arms of the Light Being reach out and you find yourself being held in the arms of total love. Soak it up. Feel and know the truth that you are so loved, so infinitely valuable, so precious. You have a special and important assignment here. This assignment is to learn to love yourself, to learn that you are part of God's expression, to learn to radiate more and more love. Beginning with your hearts, you and the Light Being merge and melt into One.

HEAL ANY HURT OR TROUBLED MEMORY FROM CHILDHOOD OR ADOLESCENCE

Relaxing exercise (described previously). 2) Bring the situation to mind and then invite the Light Being to fill it with infinite love. 3) Ask the child/adolescent what it needs to experience to be healed. What does he/she need to hear? To say? To have happen differently? Allow the Light Being to bring about that healing transforming experience. 4) Ask the Light Being to help you see your lesson or learning. Then, you the child/adolescent, and the Light Being embrace & become One.

FORGIVENESS AND RELEASE

We often tend to hang on to pain and old situations until we are "sick and tired of being sick and tired." Certainly life is process, and we must allow ourselves enough time to move through our own processes. Yet, we can delay our progress here in Earth School if we stay stuck in an unforgiving attitude. We cannot grow psychologically and spiritually unless and until we release our grievances. What is release? Release is:

- forgiving everyone and everything.
- forgiving life for taking away from us what we want to keep.
- letting go of the past, even the happy past, so we may live fully now.
- letting go of people, places things, so that everyone and everything concerned might go on to higher god.
- getting into the positive flow of life, no matter what the outer circumstances.
- opening the door of our cage of pain and resistance and walking out into free air.

When you're ready to begin releasing, an inner timer will seem to ring. The message is that it's time to get on with it. You've been angry, self-pitying, and beat down long enough! Once you've made a decision to move forward, the active forgiveness process can start. Forgiveness is a choice, an act of will, and when your own will fails, you can call upon a higher power to help you. Reaching the point of total release and forgiveness can take days, months, even years. Repeat the following exercise as many times as it takes, until there is a total feeling of love and peace toward all people (including yourself). Don't be surprised to find this may be a continuing lifetime project.

FORGIVENESS EXPERIENCE:

1) Relaxing exercise (described previously)

2) Bring to mind a person (may be you) or situation you have been unable to forgive thus far.

3) Allow emotions about the person and the situation to surface - FEEL what you really feel.

4) BE HONEST. Ask yourself, "Do I truly desire to forgive?"

5) If the answer is NO, ask for help from the Light Being. Ask to be shown how you hurt yourself when you don't forgive. If you can't move beyond unforgiveness right now, let it be. You have started a process in your consciousness that leads to change.

6) If the answer is YES, I want to forgive, say: " I TURN THIS PERSON, THIS SITUATION OVER TO THE LOVE OF GOD. I FORGIVE."

7) Continue to see the Light Being standing beside you loving and encouraging you. Now, see the bonds holding you to the person or situation or to the negativity about yourself. Examine these bonds. They may be thick as ropes or as thin as spider webs. Notice how confining they are. The Light Being now hands you a Wand of Light more powerful than a laser and instructs you to cut the bonds. You take the Wand of Light and take all the time you need to sever the bonds. Ask the Light Being to help you cut any that you have difficulty with -they drop away and disintegrate.

8) Imagine the person or situation you are now separated from surrounded by Light and Love. See the person move on to Highest Good and the situation move into total Divine Order.

9) FEEL love and light permeating your every cell - your every thought. You are in the care and keeping of LOVE. Affirm: I HAVE FORGIVEN. THE CHAINS OF UNFORGIVENESS ARE BROKEN. I AM FREE. I AM FREE WITH THE FREEDOM OF SPIRIT!

DEALING WITH GRIEF - RELEASING LOVED ONES

There is no simple easy way, no simple easy answer. Until we feel this pain for ourselves, we hope that somehow fate will spare us. I often used to wonder how people could stand the pain of losing someone they love. Then, having no choice but to stand it myself, I compared it to a madman hacking someone's arm off and running away with it. The person without the arm has no choice but to cope with it, to try to find the way to a meaningful life in spite of the loss. All too often people are expected to go on with their lives as though the loved one never existed. The grieving person is not encouraged to talk about the death or share current feelings. Some of us carry a heavy load of un-resolved grief for years. The only way to resolve it is to feel it, to finish business with the loved one and then accept the ultimate truth that there is only ongoing life. There is no specific time limit. My process took years, probably because I didn't begin to consciously deal with my pain and loss for several years after Richard's death.

You each have your own unique circumstances, your own unique time-table. It takes as long as it takes, and that's OK. The following exercises should be repeated as often as necessary.

DIALOGUE TO FINISH BUSINESS WITH LOVED ONE WHO HAS DIED

1) Relaxing exercise (described previously)

2) Say three times the name of the person who has died, and then see that person standing in front of you. The Light Being is always right there beside you.

3) Tell this person whatever is in your mind and heart. Do you have guilts? Angers? Tell the person and note the response.

4) Is there something you need to forgive this person for? Can you do it now? Is there something you need to be forgiven for? Can you feel the person forgiving you?

5) You and the loved one embrace. Feel the love that flows between you. In this moment you know that love can never die, no matter what happens to the body.

6) You, your loved one and the Light Being embrace & become One.

RELEASE LOVED ONE - DISSOLVE CHAINS OF GRIEF

1) Relaxing exercise (described previously)

2) Say three times the name of the person who has died and then see that person standing in front of you, the Light Being beside you.

3) See the bonds of pain and grief around your heart and around your loved one. (They look like chains, ropes, even spider webs.)

4) The Light Being gives you a Wand of Light stronger than a laser and tells you to cut these bonds. See and feel yourself doing this. If you need help, this loving Being of Light helps you.

5) The bonds fall away so that only light and love flow between you and your loved one. Your heart feels expanded. The weight is lifting.

6) Now, the loved one and his/her Being of Light are going together up a stairway. You realize that it is not yet time for you to travel up this stairway.

7) You now release this person you love to go on to Higher Realms. You see that this person is totally safe, loved and cared for.

8) Continue to feel the love connection between you. You understand that you can communicate with the person, ask to feel the love of this person, anytime you need to.

COSMIC PERSPECTIVE

When we drop the earth suit we call our physical body, I believe that our soul has an opportunity to evaluate our experience here in Earth School this time around. We look at our successes and our failures and see the overall pattern. Then, along with a totally loving Light Being, we set up the lessons for the next earthly embodiment. We all choose the difficulty of each life. Some pack the growth intensity of several lifetimes into one. Others may choose an easier path. I believe that we choose conditions, parents, relationships, and life goals before we're born. Souls tend to incarnate together, meeting and learning by previous agreement. We change roles; man, woman, parent, child, race and social conditions. There are those advanced souls who are free to move on to higher dimensions, but who nevertheless choose to come to earth to be a guiding light for others. Others continue to work from the invisible realm for our evolution. Our assignment then, is to learn our lesson of love - to live in love - to BE love - to enter full time into the Kingdom of Heaven. We have as many lifetimes as it takes. The choice is ours.

LIFE REVIEW

1) Relaxing exercise (described previously)

2) Make a list of the most important people and the major events of your life. Include those people that you embrace and those that you resist. Include successes and accomplishments as well as disappointments and failures. Leave some spaces between each entry. Be sure to include parents, children, husbands, wives, lovers - any person who has played a significant role in your life.

3) Go down the list one person/one event at a time and with the aid of your Light Being, record the lesson/s you have learned from each person and each event.
4) Take note of the people or events that call out for your forgiveness and release. Be aware that your soul chose these people and events so that you could learn the lesson of love.

5) Look into the eyes of your Being of Light and be open and receptive to the love that is now being poured out to you. You are told, "You are totally loved and accepted. There is nothing you have ever done that could take this love away. There is nothing you have ever done that could bring more love to you. You already are totally and completely loved - you are LOVE."

6) Now, with your true identity established, send Love and Light to every person and every event in your life, bless each person and each event for the learning you received. Know that there has always been DIVINE ORDER in your life.

7) Turn and face your Light Being. Your hearts begin to expand and then you merge together and become ONE.

THE BLESSINGS OF GOD REST UPON YOU;
PEACE ABIDES WITH YOU.
THE PRESENCE ILLUMINATES YOUR HEART
NOW AND FOREVERMORE.
AMEN.

RECOMMENDED READING and STUDY

Course in Miracles - Foundation for Inner Peace

A New Earth - Eckhart Tolle

Discover the Power Within You & In the Flow of Life - Eric Butterworth

Eye of the I - David Hawkins

What We May Be - Pierro Ferruci

A Diamond in Your Pocket - Gangaji

God Speaks - Meher Baba

The Untethered Soul - Michael A. Singer

AUTHOR CONTACT

Julie Ireland Keene is available for speaking engagements, workshops, retreats, in small in-home groups, and telephone counseling. She may be contacted at Jewelskeene613@aol.com Phone 513-254-0238 website: Jewelskeenespirit.com

About the Author

Julie Ireland Keene has served several Unity ministries. Before becoming a minister, she was a professor of Language and Literature at Ferris State University in Michigan. She travels extensively throughout the United States, sharing her spiritual journey of overcoming. Her purpose is to inspire, support and coach those who are searching for a path that leads to peace, love, joy, and fulfillment.